Blueprint Small

Blueprint Small

Creative Ways
to Live with Less

Michelle Kodis

GIBBS SMITH

Gibbs Smith, Publisher
Salt Lake City

Dedication:

For Richard, who makes everything possible.

Call for Submissions

Blueprint Small #2 is now in the works, and we welcome your ideas and submissions. If you know of a great house that is small and creatively designed, please tell us about it. The space must be 1,500 square feet or less.

Send submissions to:
Michelle Kodis
P.O. Box 3962
Telluride, CO 81435
or email: kodis@independence.net

First Edition
07 06 05 04 03 5 4 3 2 1

Text © 2003 by Michelle Kodis
Photographs © as noted throughout

Published by
Gibbs Smith, Publisher
P.O. Box 667
Layton, Utah 84041

Orders: (1-800) 748-5439
www.gibbs-smith.com

Project directed by Suzanne Gibbs Taylor
Edited by Monica Millward Weeks
Designed and produced by Kurt Wahlner
Printed and bound in Hong Kong

Library of Congress Cataloging-in-Publication Data
Kodis, Michelle.
Blueprint small : creative ways to live with less / Michelle Kodis.—1st ed.
p. cm.
ISBN 1-58685-175-6
1. Architecture, Domestic—United States. 2. Architecture—United States—20th century. I. Title.
NA7208 .K63 2003
728'.3—dc21
                                        2002015982

Acknowledgments

My gratitude and thanks to:

The architects, designers, homeowners, photographers, and other professionals, whose input, cooperation, suggestions, and boundless creativity are evident on every page of this book.

Gibbs Smith, a publisher who believes that books can change the world.

Suzanne Taylor, an editor with the rare ability to give a writer that matchless combination of guidance and artistic freedom.

Robert, Joan, and Steven Kodis, my beloved family.

The friends who provide perspective and laughs: Kendall Yaw Cieciuch, Marcia Cohen, Mary Duffy, Donna Fecteau, Ramona Gaylord, Susanna Hoffman, Jean Koch, Louise Redd, Susan Smilanic-Simpson, Susannah Smith, Rosemerry Wahtola Trommer, and Susan Viebrock.

Andrew and Brett Cieciuch, who remind me to play.

Contents

Introduction

Chicago, Illinois;
Venice, California;
Chicago, Illinois.

Berkeley, California.

SOMETHING CAUGHT MY EYE one day as I was flipping through a real estate magazine. One of the properties featured encompassed some 36,000 square feet. Included in the home's floor plan were ten bedrooms, fourteen bathrooms, a master suite, an indoor pool, a theater, a wine cellar, a guesthouse, caretaker's quarters, and parking spaces for more than ten vehicles. A few weeks later, I came across an article about a 295-square-foot home built on a postage-stamp-sized lot in Tokyo. Lauded for its resourceful use of extremely limited space, this house vividly demonstrated that a comfortable, livable home is not necessarily born out of square footage.

The contrast between these two dwellings is clear, but beyond their differences in size we discover something ultimately more provocative: What is enough space? Is "enough" related more to dimensions or to how a particular space is used and enjoyed? Do large homes meet the basic needs of their inhabitants—or, more pointedly, can they? Are people drawn to smaller homes because, in the best of circumstances, they aim to invite rather than overwhelm?

9

The responses to these questions would most likely be as varied as the individuals giving the answers. Still, many people feel an undeniable attraction to well-planned and thoughtfully arranged small spaces. Advocates of living small believe that this philosophy, which is straightforward by nature, reminds us of the emotional appeal of cozy, intelligently conceived rooms, creative and efficient ways to store belongings, and structures that encourage a strong connection to community and the environment. The singular rule underlying this philosophy is simple: All the space is used. In many cases, people who live in very large homes tend to gravitate toward certain key areas of the house, leaving the other rooms to sit vacant. Notes cultural anthropologist Susanna Hoffman, who has studied the living habits of diverse societies, "Americans in particular tend to think they need large spaces, and yet they often end up living in just a few rooms. Most people around the world live in small spaces. As humans, we nest. We seek coziness."

Even so, the reality is that the American home has been expanding, and along with that, its "footprint"—the amount of land it requires. Today, the median size of a single-family home is around 2,100 square feet, whereas in 1967 it was closer to 1,500 square feet. According to the U.S. Census Bureau, in 1987, 13 percent of new homes were 1,200 square feet or less, but by 2000, only 6 percent of homes were that small. Similarly, in 1987, 21 percent of newly constructed homes were 2,400 square feet or larger; by 2000, that figure had risen to 35 percent. Nonetheless, a parallel trend is steadily emerging, shaped by the premise that scaling back, choosing a smaller home and, by default, a smaller footprint, and treating one's living space as a piece of the whole, rather than as a separate entity, can be the more desirable alternative.

In this book, you'll find that people's attitudes toward living small are as unique as their personalities. From a sleek high-rise apartment in an urban center to a playful studio added to a suburban house, the projects presented here invite you to explore inspiring and imaginative ways to build and appoint small spaces. Although the structures themselves are architecturally distinct, each illustrates a fundamental theme: Small spaces, whether primary living quarters or places for retreat or work, can be wonderful options to endless square footage. The owners of these buildings, as well as the architects behind their design and construction, speak a language that is becoming increasingly prevalent among people of all walks of life: It is the language of fresh ideas about how we live today and also how we measure our collective impact on the planet. The small house movement involves, sometimes by design, sometimes by necessity, the process of simplification: purging excess, paring down to the essentials, and carving out extra physical and psychological room for living.

The small spaces in this book represent a spectrum of locations, budgets and individual style and taste, but all were chosen because they prove that scaling back doesn't have to become a sacrifice in comfort, spaciousness, or beauty. You might be reading this book because you are ready to create your own small space. Or, you could still be in the dreaming stages—envisioning a home or room that meets your needs and makes your heart do a little leap when you walk into it. I hope the examples in this book will foster your dreams, give you workable and interesting ideas, and make you smile.

MICHELLE KODIS

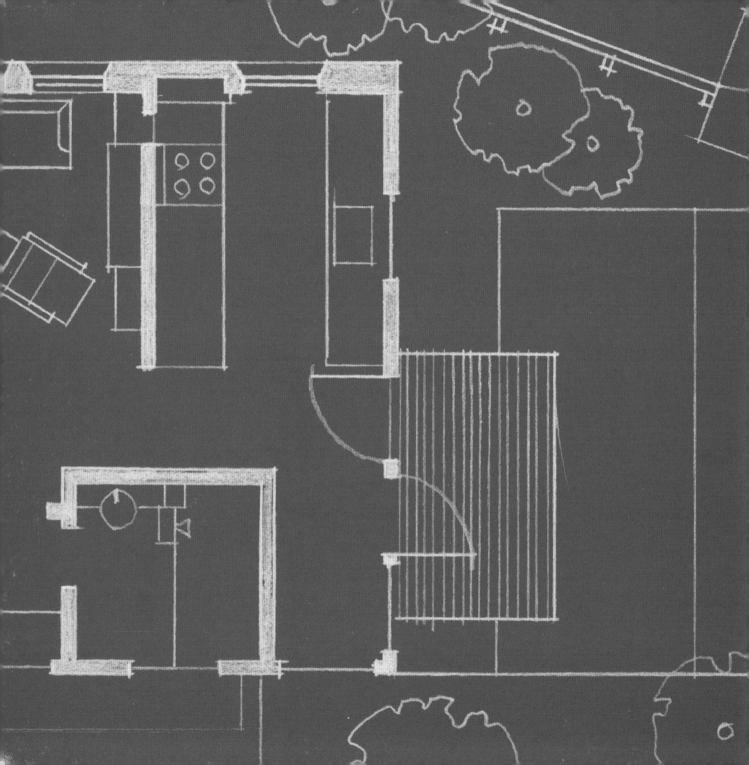

1

*Merging indoor and outdoor living spaces
imparts a light–filled
expansiveness to a Venice bungalow.*

The Joys of California Living

Size: 750 square feet

Architect: Steven Shortridge,
Callas Shortridge Architects

Photographs: Claudio Santini

Lush landscaping lining the perimeter of the
garden fence maximizes privacy, as does the
steel-plate fireplace wall located adjacent to
comfortable built-in seating. A mahogany outdoor dining table, designed by the owner, is
perfect for dinner parties.

Item of Interest:
The outdoor living room's
teak-and-aluminum chaise
lounge is by Spanish designer
Gandia Blasco.

SOUTHERN CALIFORNIA'S temperate climate is a
solid argument in itself for living small. Here,
where the temperatures are shirtsleeve pleasant for
a good part of the year, the limited square footage
of a small home can be made to seem like much
more when the outdoors are integrated into the
primary living spaces.

Architect Steven Shortridge has done exactly that
in his 750-square-foot bungalow in Venice,
California. Not content just to remodel the
interior, which he did over a six-month period,
Shortridge also turned his savvy design eye toward
the home's back garden that was, in his mind, one
of its most appealing aspects. Although the home
was a hodgepodge of seemingly unrelated boxy
rooms that included a parlor, dining area, and
kitchen but no proper bedroom, the presence of
the unlandscaped yard captured Shortridge's
imagination. Aside from acting as a buffer from

the busy pedestrian area (the home is bordered by alleys on three sides), Shortridge believed the garden held the potential to become a key part of the overall floor plan without too much of an overhaul. Today, it is a functional extension of the house. In this well-used outdoor living room, he explains, "the sky is the ceiling."

Shortridge bought the house in 1996. Originally part of a grander Hollywood home, it was moved to its current site in 1937, most likely to be used as a weekend retreat. Vacant for nearly a decade when the architect found it, the house was in what

Formerly part of a larger home, the house now resides in a pedestrian-focused area of Venice Beach. Pigmented plaster lends vibrant color to the property and is also a material that will stand up to time. The original stucco exterior had a textured quality, but the architect wanted a smoother, more updated look. To achieve this, he employed a steel-trowel process that trimmed up the edges and freshened the outside walls. The tranquil home is set apart from its urban environment by extensive landscaping, including a variety of fruit and palm trees, bamboo, and a sturdy but elegant fence made of concrete panels and translucent fiberglass.

Venice Bungalow

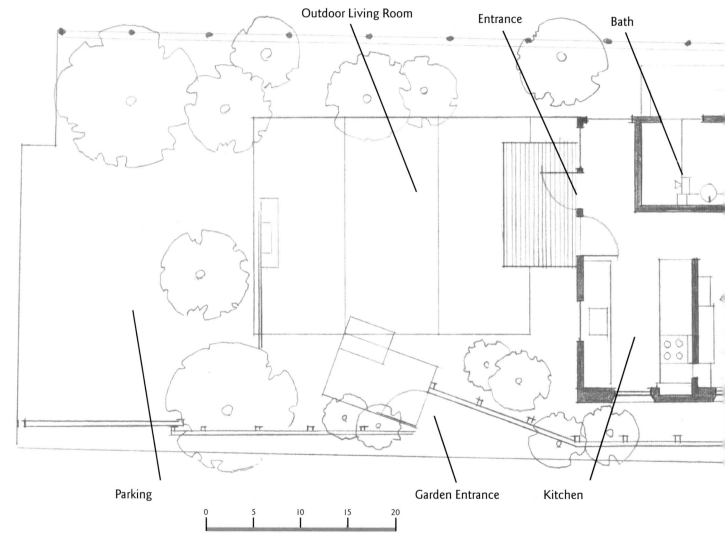

Outdoor Living Room

Entrance

Bath

Parking

Garden Entrance

Kitchen

Scale: $^1/_2$" equals 5'

0   5   10   15   20

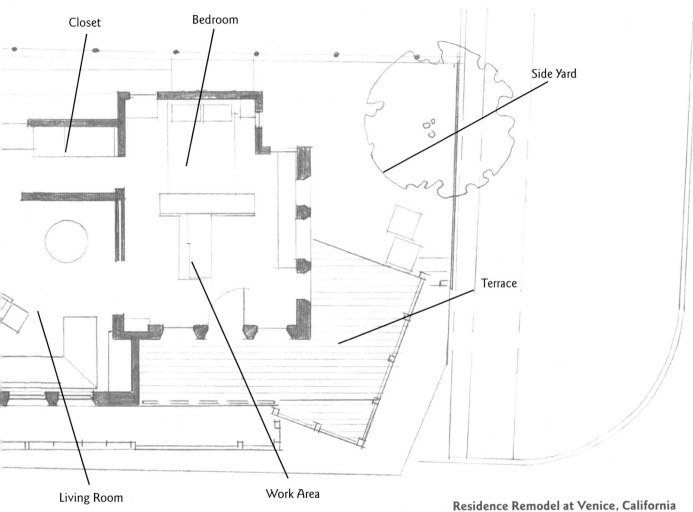

Closet

Bedroom

Side Yard

Living Room

Work Area

Terrace

Residence Remodel at Venice, California

750 Square Feet

Architect: Steven Shortridge, Callas Shortridge Architects

he describes as "a good bad old state—it was falling apart, but it hadn't been poorly renovated either, so there were nice features still left."

As he honed his remodeling plan, the architect paid special attention to issues of connectivity and light flow. "The garden affected how I redid the house and also how I worked to create a connection to it," he says. "When you're dealing with a very small space, you are faced with the continual challenge of how to use every square inch of that space in a meaningful way. Connecting the outside to the inside accomplished this, and expanded the feeling of the whole house."

Shortridge focused on reorienting the home toward the garden. Prior to the remodel, the path from the inside of the house to the garden had been cumbersome: one had to pass through two sets of doors in the laundry room to get to it. To create a more graceful and inviting course, the architect relocated the main entrance to

An aluminum-and-fiberglass awning links the indoor and outdoor living areas, and generously proportioned French-style doors form a spacious new entry into the home. An eighteen-inch raised concrete pad brings the outdoor living room closer to the main level of the house, fostering continuity between the two spaces, which are joined by three substantial mahogany steps.

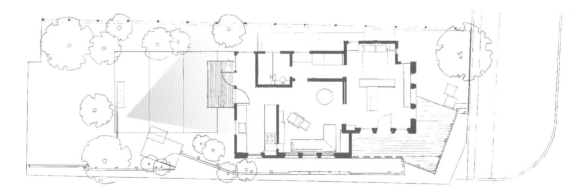

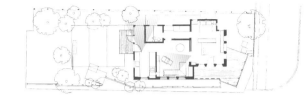

The home's minimal entry hall is an eye-pleasing transition into the house from the garden. Accessed via French-style doors, it has room for an Eames chair and a painting by Sam Messer. Stained oak flooring contrasts nicely with the orange window trim.

The cabinet and mirror, which were in the original home, provide clutter-free storage and a contrast to the home's contemporary furnishings. Placing mirrors in small rooms can create the illusion of a larger space, as is evident here. The narrow wall slot to the left of the cabinet is part of a door now partially closed off; the architect opted to keep the opening because it creates a sense of continuity between the individual spaces.

Item of Interest:
The "grasshopper" chair in the indoor living room area is by Eero Saarinen and is currently available through Modernica stores in Los Angeles and Manhattan.

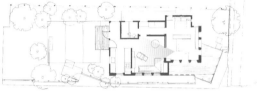

Natural light fills the home, thanks in large part to a reworked floor plan that now flows in an unrestricted manner. Manipulating ceiling heights also changed the interior personality of the house dramatically. Here, a raised portion of the ceiling, clad in tongue-and-groove Douglas fir, is lit up by strategically placed and space-conscious cove-lighting fixtures.

Item of Interest:
The ant chairs in the dining area are by Arnie Jacobson.

the side of the property. The garden's surrounding privacy-screen walls, made of concrete panels and translucent fiberglass, hold a gate on one side that serves as the primary access.

For the outdoor living room, Shortridge replaced the home's back door with French-style doors that face the garden. He then poured an eighteen-inch concrete pad for a floor and installed three mahogany steps that lead up to the house. A wing-like awning of translucent fiberglass panels set into an aluminum frame protects the doors, catches and diverts rainwater away from the patio, is a filter for natural light, and is the official bridge

Colorful contemporary paintings by Sam Messer complement the restored Douglas fir sliding pocket door, which was present in the original house. The door separates the sleeping/work area from the living room/dining area and, because it slides rather than opens out, is also a space-saving alternative to a traditional door.

Tall windows face an alley located just several feet away on the other side of the garden wall. Thanks to the privacy fence, the large mullion-free windows can remain uncovered, a simple design measure that maximizes ambient light and further emphasizes the connection between the home's inside and outside living spaces.

The kitchen appliances are compact to keep the space in proportion to the rest of the house. The architect employed a creative trick with the skylight, placing half of it over the kitchen and the other half over the adjacent bathroom. "Splitting" the skylight in this manner creates an unexpected expansion of space and sends light down into both rooms.

With its original tiles and window and trim detail, the kitchen is the most untouched part of the house. The additional space created via the outdoor living room meant the kitchen could remain small without compromising the home's livability.

between the house and the garden. "The awning adds to the transition from the inside to the outside," Shortridge explains. "It opens up and out into the outdoor living room. It's a true link." Realizing that the water heater and washer and dryer were taking up too much room inside, he transferred them to an exterior side of the house.

Inside, Shortridge employed a number of inventive techniques that allowed him to free the house from its unwieldy floor plan and retain the more attractive elements of the house, such as the baseboards, window trim, and a Douglas fir sliding pocket door that now divides the two main interior spaces—the living/dining room and the bedroom/office. Not wanting to obliterate the home's history, the architect was careful to preserve these "stronger" components, "mixing some of the old with the contemporary additions," he explains.

Tapping into his keen understanding of what small spaces need to come alive, Shortridge transformed the interior with a number of visually striking design measures whose combined effect is one of greater depth and expansiveness. To illustrate, the ceilings in the home were eight feet—too low and "dark," in the architect's opinion. To convey a more voluminous mood, he raised portions of the ceilings to ten feet and finished them in Douglas fir to match the original window material. Ambient light flow is encouraged through a new skylight placed over the shower and a clerestory window positioned above the bed.

Lack of adequate storage is an all-too-frequent reality in many small homes, and the challenge is to find ways to add storage areas that don't consume precious square footage and blend with the interior scheme. Shortridge faced this problem to the extreme—his house had no closets. He discovered his solution in built-in cabinetry, a smart and popular

technique for tight spaces. For example, the dressing hall between the bedroom and the bathroom now contains a compartmentalized built-in dresser that provides ample room for clothes and doesn't intrude into the space as a regular closet would. Made of medium-density fiberboard and Douglas fir veneer, the dresser is a stylishly compact option.

Any home's success depends on how well it matches and facilitates the lifestyle of its occupants, and this Venice gem passes that test with flair. "I've been able to use the out-door living room every month of the year," Shortridge is pleased to say. "Even in an urban setting, I get to enjoy a beautiful and private environment on an everyday basis."

Originally the living room/parlor, the recon-figured and combined bedroom and work area illustrates the benefits of leaving a space unwalled and only partially separated. This allows the rooms to merge while still serving their individual functions.

31

The bathroom is separated from the bedroom area by a short "dressing hall" and a sliding pocket door. A slim green tile wall on one side of the combination tub/shower provides a decorative way to disguise plumbing. A sleek built-in cabinet made of affordable medium-density fiberboard (MDF) and covered in Douglas fir veneer is tucked into the hallway.

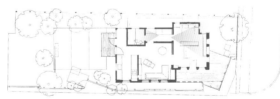

A tall bookcase defines the sleeping area, where a portion of the ceiling has been removed and raised up to accommodate a clerestory window, a simple feature that does an excellent job of imparting a sense of spaciousness.

2

Inexpensive but architecturally creative materials and a nod to local heritage coexist harmoniously in a small space with a big heart.

A Cost-Efficient
Caretaker Apartment

Size: 900 square feet

Architect: Larry Yaw,
Cottle Graybeal Yaw Architects

Photographs: Patrick Sudmeier

The eye-pleasing possibilities of "urban camouflage" are apparent here, where blocks of green paint break up the white expanse of the building and create interesting color proportions.

ARCHITECT LARRY YAW is accustomed to working with clients with big budgets and dreams of high-end custom homes; his ability to design beautifully appointed and architecturally distinct houses has earned him numerous recognitions, including Colorado Architect of the Year in 2001 and selection to *Architectural Digest*'s "AD100." But when it came time for Yaw, who is a principal in the Basalt, Colorado–based firm of Cottle Graybeal Yaw Architects, to build for himself and his wife, he turned away from custom and headed straight for the everyday. His self-imposed goal: create a comfortable and workable living space using inexpensive easy-to-find materials in innovative ways that are even easier on the wallet. "I wanted to challenge myself with the notion of using common elements taken off the shelf in uncommon ways," he says. "With this house, I wanted to be able to go to the lumber store and get everything there."

For his own personal approach to small, Yaw looked to the classic example of efficient space: the sailboat. "Sailboats are models of flexibility and smart storage," he says. "When you set out to build small, it changes your perspective. In many ways, it's like boat building: everything begins with focusing at a reduced scale." The result of Yaw's efforts is a light and airy one-bedroom caretaker garage apartment that served as the Yaws' residence for two years while the couple remodeled a larger home on the site. This experiment in "sailboat" living has been so successful that Yaw says he wouldn't mind staying in the apartment permanently. "When you have the challenge of designing a small space on a budget, you have to apply different levels of innovation," he says. "Small projects make you think differently. You can throw money at any problem, but if you throw creative thought at it instead, then the artistic, functional, and eco-nomic aspects of the project come together in new ways. Simple design can make a difference. You don't need fancy stuff—you need quality of space."

The property is landscaped with a number of terraced benches, and the apartment is located on the highest of those benches and configured on two levels so that the upper living spaces (the living and dining areas and the kitchen) can take advantage of treetop views. Strongly influenced by the simple honesty of rural building forms and also by the Victorian architecture that

From this view, the apartment looks out over a series of terraced yards and appears far more spacious than its 900 square feet would indicate. Plenty of windows, a balcony, and a covered deck merge the interior and exterior spaces, creating a connection to the beautiful tree-rich site. Painted cedar shingles in the gable continue the historic dairy farm design theme, and a painted steel sunscreen shades the upper-level living room and a small porch.

Colorado Caretaker

North Elevation

East Elevation

South Elevation

Entry Level

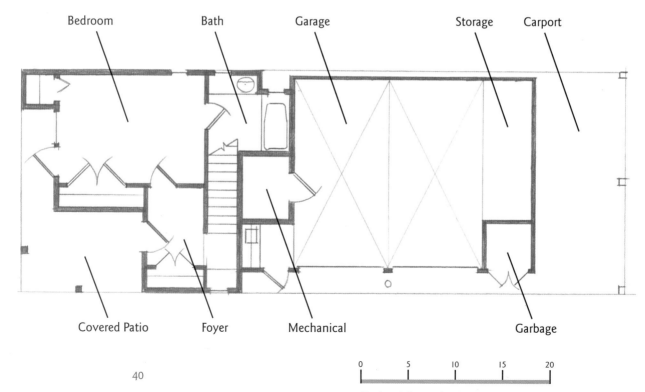

Bedroom

Bath

Garage

Storage

Carport

Covered Patio

Foyer

Mechanical

Garbage

Scale: $^1/_2$" equals 5'

0   5   10   15   20

Upper Level

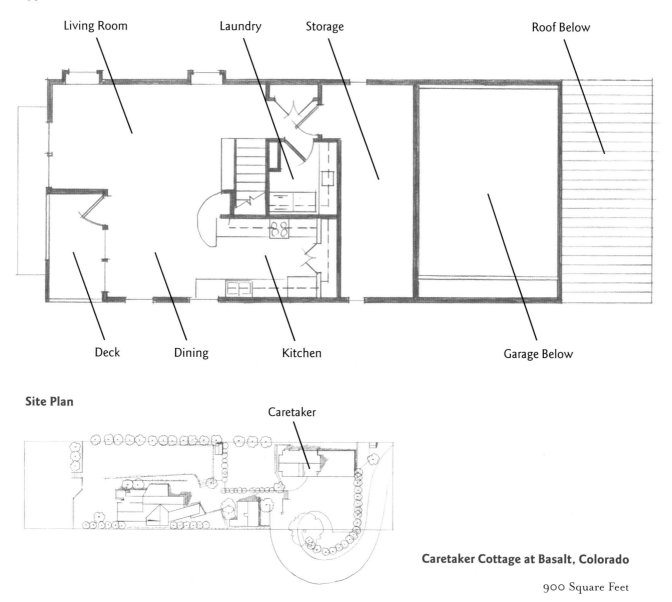

Living Room

Laundry

Storage

Roof Below

Deck

Dining

Kitchen

Garage Below

Site Plan

Caretaker

Caretaker Cottage at Basalt, Colorado

900 Square Feet

Architect: Larry Yaw, Cottle Graybeal Yaw Architects

The recessed garage and entry add variation to the length of the building. A green-painted dormer adds height and visual interest. Stained and brushed concrete, an inexpensive and durable material, serves as the garage apron and caretaker entry.

A dramatically sloping galvanized-metal shed roof emerges from the north-side gable, which is covered in painted cedar shingles. In addition to its architectural appeal, the shed roof creates a reduced, comfortable neighborhood scale from the street approach.

Plenty of windows and a small porch bring natural light into the room, imparting a spacious feel far beyond the implied limits of the actual square footage. Straightforward materials, such as a board-and-batten ceiling and painted drywall, add to the clean uncluttered personality of the space.

characterizes old Basalt, the apartment relates to the property's early-1900s farming heritage, borrowing from the dairy farm theme primarily in the creative use of color to delineate exterior elements. Yaw selected a palette of varying shades of green and used blocks of color as a graphic contrast to the building's white exterior. In Yaw's terms, the green acts as "urban camouflage" by visually breaking up the surface planes of the house. "Otherwise, it would be an imposing white mass," he points out, adding that this effect can be achieved on a frugal budget.

Inside the apartment, Yaw played with the open floor plan, "creating habitation out of found spaces." One such found space was a storage area that, because Yaw had the forethought to give it a window, can double as an extra bedroom or a work area. Additional space beneath the stairs became a tiny lavatory, and the storage space under the sloping roof houses cabinets and a pantry. The storage room's dimensions were specially designed to accommodate large plastic storage bins—crucial to Yaw, an avid outdoorsman who owns an extensive collection of sports gear and needed somewhere to organize it. All of these are further examples of the shipbuilding mentality that Yaw adopted as his guiding principle.

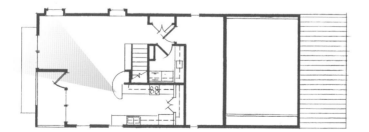

In keeping with one of the basic rules of well-built small spaces, the stairway is tucked tightly into the floor plan.

The bedroom is big enough to accommodate a large bed that was custom-designed by Yaw for a former home. This was made possible through the use of built-in cabinetry, which eliminates the need for a space-taking piece of furniture.

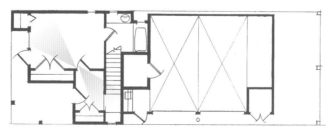

One of the most noteworthy aspects of the apartment is that Yaw was able to build it for about $130 per square foot—an impressive feat in Basalt, which neighbors expensive Aspen and has felt the effects of the resort's high cost of living and building. The kitchen area is an inspiring example of how inexpensive can look far from ordinary when done the right way. Cost-saving materials include cabinets made of banded fir plywood equipped with cutouts instead of traditional handles to avoid hardware costs, counters coated in budget-conscious plastic laminate, and open shelves of painted wood. Not wanting to waste any space, Yaw added a simple breakfast nook that can also serve as a worktable—another example of the double-duty aspect of living in small spaces, an important design tactic that maximizes a compact floor plan. Inexpensive materials are also found in the living room, which features a rough-sawn plywood cedar board-and-batten ceiling, an affordable element that imparts "a rural texture inexpensively," Yaw explains. The walls are basic drywall with wood trim. In the lower-level bedroom, built-in drawers made of pre-finished melamine remove the need for a separate piece of furniture, thus saving precious space.

Yaw believes that small spaces work best when they "merge" to envelop all aspects of living—from working and playing to eating and relaxing. "If well designed, areas can 'live' together—the kitchen, living room, bedroom," he explains. "When you separate spaces, you separate people, and design that connects people to place and, more importantly, to each other is one of my primary design premises. The concept of 'home' is central to our well-being. It's important to feel connected to that sanctuary."

The kitchen features a board-and-batten ceiling, which lends a rustic ambience to the room. The space is light-filled, thanks to generous windows and the use of white paint throughout. Plywood cabinets have cutout handles instead of hardware—a cost-cutting move that also adds a contemporary touch. The clean lines of the room are continued in the open shelves and in the elegant curve of the breakfast nook. Although the materials were inexpensive, the effect is reminiscent of products from the higher end of the building and design spectrum.

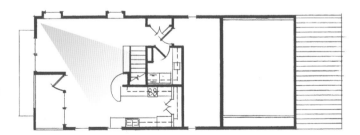

The consistent use of color can bring highly pleasing results. Here, a horizontal board-and-batten wall painted dark green creates an inviting nook for a simple bench.

Whimsy never hurts, and here, a Corinthian column painted green adds an element of surprise to the house. Columns have been incorporated into all of the Yaw family homes; this one was found in a South Carolina opera house.

3

Graceful lines and site–sensitive design meet in a pool/guest house that blends into its wooded setting and is a peaceful place to relax and enjoy nature.

An Elegant
Suburban Retreat

Size: 920 square feet

Architect: Jeff Blackledge, Archimania

Photographs: Jeffrey Jacobs

The tapered end beams of the cypress trellis balance the structure, preventing it from appearing too bulky and heavy for the clean lines of the façade. The gable roof features a ridge that extends eighteen inches beyond the roof fascia, an architectural technique that makes the roof seem as if it is floating. Copper lights on either side of the French doors convey a Craftsman-style feel.

THE CITY OF MEMPHIS, Tennessee, is only a short drive away, but this pool/guest house in a neighborhood about twenty miles from downtown feels far removed from anything remotely urban.

When architect Jeff Blackledge was called upon to design the structure, which sits behind a main house, he was given two fundamental guidelines: distinguish the pool house from the primary residence and minimize the impact of construction. Blackledge took these cues to heart and conceived a small house that is elegantly proportioned, speaks of a down-to-earth materiality, and is sensitively tuned in to its heavily wooded terrain, which slopes steeply and terminates some thirty-five feet down a hill at an adjoining wilderness preserve that parallels the Wolf River and is home to deer, birds, and other animals.

While studying the site, Blackledge began to envision a tall narrow house. His logic was that building up rather than out would reduce the overall footprint, thus keeping construction as low-key as possible and also creating an architectural contrast to the more traditionally appointed Georgian-style main house. The home's compact floor plan consists of three levels: a 120-square-foot sleeping loft, a 500-square-foot middle-level living room/dining/kitchen area that looks out onto the pool, and a 300-square-foot basement with a bedroom and an exercise room. The levels are linked via a spiral staircase and a loft ladder, and the result is a versatile space that is comfortable and family-friendly. "Even though it's small, there are many different experiences to be had in this house because of the levels and the foreground views," Blackledge notes.

The home's tight vertical dimensions also saved precious trees. Blackledge literally designed the house to fit in between its woodland neighbors, in one instance going so far as to extract a notch on the west side of the house so that a nearby tree would not be disturbed during the digging of the foundation. Lifting a section of the mid-level floor and supporting it with posts rather than allowing it to extend to the ground meant that the tree's delicate root system was left unharmed. This site-conscious measure brought yet another benefit to the exterior:

Dramatic windows trimmed in metal that has been painted in a warm gray tint, together with an exaggerated gable roof, impart a contemporary character to the front side of the pool/guest house. A cypress trellis, an artistic way to soften the tall façade, shades the deck from the sun and serves as a transition between the building's indoor and outdoor zones. The trellis also lends a human scale to the house and links it contextually to its lush setting.

Memphis Pool House

Basement Plan

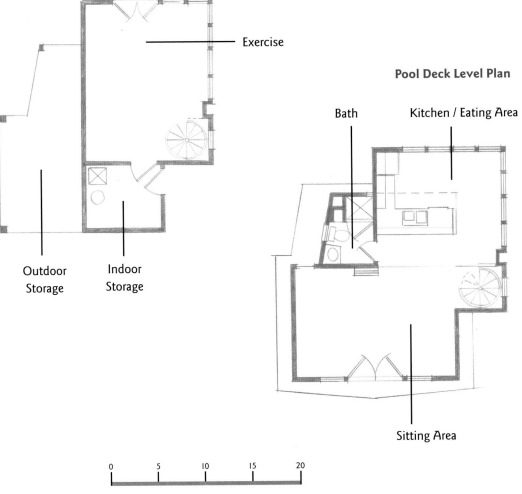

Exercise

Pool Deck Level Plan

Bath

Kitchen / Eating Area

Outdoor Storage

Indoor Storage

Sitting Area

0   5   10   15   20

Scale: $^{1}/_{2}$" equals 5'

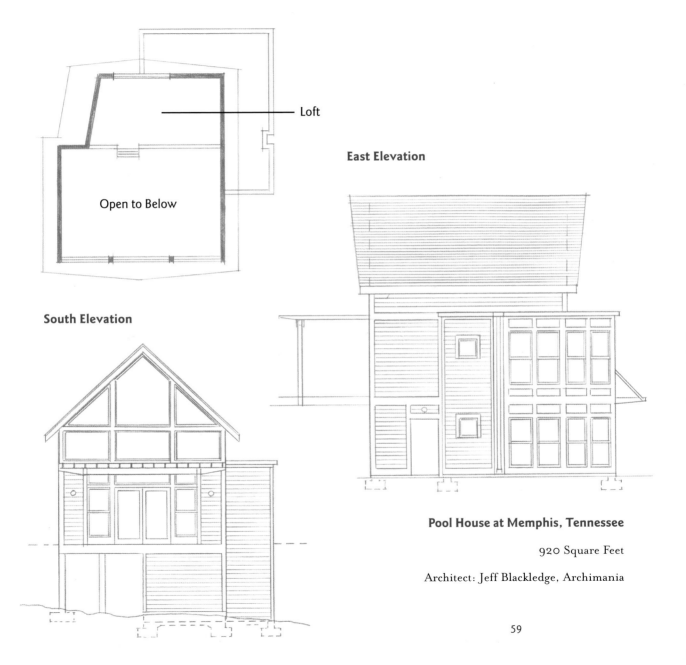

Loft Level Plan

Loft

Open to Below

East Elevation

South Elevation

Pool House at Memphis, Tennessee

920 Square Feet

Architect: Jeff Blackledge, Archimania

a touch of unexpected geometric surprise. Stained cypress lap siding pulls the house even further into its environment. The cypress adds texture and will eventually age into a subtle gray patina that is reminiscent of the bark of the surrounding trees. "We faced a creative and challenging siting process, namely because we didn't want to lose trees," Blackledge says. "Our goal was to maintain a strong connection to nature." This connection is encouraged, too, by an intentional lack of landscaping. While the gardens around the main house are manicured and controlled, the pool/guest house resides in an

The two box forms that comprise the house interlock to create the illusion of depth. The shower area of the bathroom is defined on the exterior by a vertical strip of glass block added to allow in light and to supply a decidedly modern detail. The notch to the right of the house pulls the structure away from a nearby tree, which was saved thanks to this quirky solution. The large triangle window in the home's top gable matches the window on the front of the house, fostering a "see-through" effect.

60

The differences between the two ends of the house are evident here: the front is airy and open while the back appears more rooted to the ground. The vertical pop-out on the east wall houses a spiral staircase and is accentuated by two small windows that break up the mass and begin the transition to the prominent window pattern that follows. The flat roof interlocks with the gabled roof, resulting in the interplay of traditional and contemporary forms. Now golden in color, the cypress siding will slowly age into a gray tone.

untamed section of the property where native plants grow freely.

The differing personalities of the front and the back of the house reveal the architect's desire to mix contemporary and traditional elements. The front, for example, showcases an updated façade with bold window placement and an exaggerated gable roof, while the back, with its quaint window layout and understated roof, is softer and has a cabin-like quality. However, both the front and the back of the house feature a triangular window on the upper-level gable—a detail that joins the two styles and spreads sunlight through the interior. Blackledge felt it was crucial that the pool house be oriented toward the outdoors. To achieve that, he positioned the floor plan to take full advantage of the beautiful surroundings. "This is meant to be an engaging and open space," Blackledge says. "The windows create a sense of transparency and invitation, and train the eye outward."

Blackledge employed another trick to impart an organic quality to the home: he extended the gable roof ridge to "give the house movement, so that it's not just a stagnant gable with a window." Here, aestheticism and pragmatism converge harmoniously: in addition to its visually pleasing form, the extended gable offers protection from the sun. Inside, the materials were kept simple and include oak floors and inexpensive Sheetrock walls. "The materials are somewhat utilitarian and standard, nothing exotic. The owners wanted the house to be maintenance-free as well as simple and straightforward," he explains.

Blackledge acknowledges that the pool-house project spoke to his own fondness for homes that have just enough room. "I prefer small spaces because they make you live more precisely and think about what you maintain and store," he says. "And, because they are more intimate and connected to the outside world, you are forced to think about your surroundings. A little space naturally forges a relationship to the environment around it."

Soaring windows kept free of coverings forge a connection between the interior and exterior spaces. The basic wood materials used inside the home refer to its natural palette without being too rustic. The railing is a simple form with plain vertical pickets to strengthen the verticality of the space.

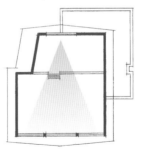

63

The family-oriented living room and dining/kitchen areas share the middle level of the house, and both have a clear view of the pool. French doors open to the deck and can be pulled back to merge the two spaces. The granite countertop is a durable and rich accent to the room.

The loft is easily accessed via an attached ladder and, because the house is set so close to the trees, it is reminiscent of a tree house. Space-saving recessed lighting adds to the light coming in from outside and brings out the luster of the heart-pine flooring.

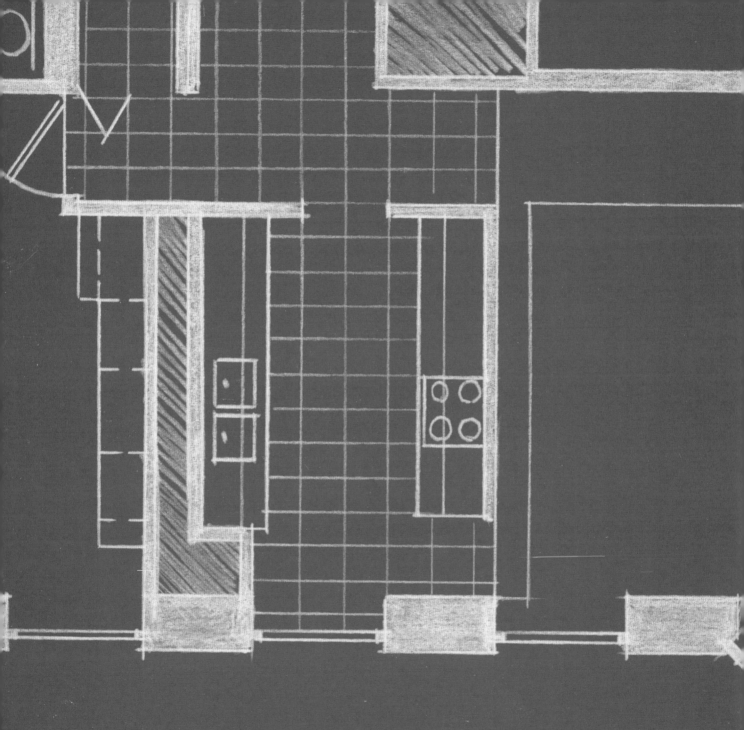

4

*How a simple reconfiguration of space and
the use of elegant eye-pleasing materials
transformed a downtown Chicago apartment.*

Tranquility
Above the Crowds

Size: 1,600 square feet

Architect: Brad Lynch,
Brininstool + Lynch Architects

Photographs: Claudio Santini

This view from the bedroom shows how opening the glass panel doors lends an inviting feel to the floor plan, making it appear much larger than it is. The glass has been laminated for a softening effect, and the steel frame is painted in a semi-gloss to achieve this look, as well.

Not long ago, Steven Liska was living in a 5,000-square-foot loft in downtown Chicago. It was a vast space for one person, but Liska liked the indoor trees and waterfall, and it provided plenty of room for his belongings. Then, something in Liska shifted, and the loft began to lose its appeal. "For one, I got tired of maintaining it," he says, "and then I decided to make a drastic change: scale back and live more simply."

That change involved selling the loft, giving away a lot of furniture, and then moving into a 1,600-square-foot condominium apartment located on the thirtieth floor of a sixty-story high-rise on Chicago's Michigan Avenue. Liska says this dramatic downsizing changed his life for the better. "I thought it would be hard, but the truth is that when you're in a larger space, you tend to spend a lot of time in the same room anyway," he says.

Liska, who is single and runs a thriving graphic-design and corporate-communications firm, wanted his new home to be relatively maintenance-free and serve as a tranquil retreat after his fast-paced days at work. However, the apartment's original interior was the exact opposite of what he envisioned. A devoted minimalist, he wanted an open floor plan, clean lines, sophistication combined with warmth—and not one unnecessary embellishment. Pre-remodel, the apartment was, as architect Brad Lynch of Chicago-based Brininstool + Lynch describes it, "full of chintz and a lot of ticky-tacky moldings—it was not very attractive. Creating a pure and minimalist space is difficult to do in this kind of building. We had to analyze the conditions there and fool with them—how could we align them to create the perception of more space?" Liska's description of the interior is perhaps not as diplomatic: "When I moved into it, it looked like a Vegas bordello," he recalls. "It was gaudy and uniquely not my style, but I bought it for the good views and the location."

Because the apartment is a corner unit, its floor plan is oddly shaped. This fact presented Lynch with the primary challenge of rethinking the transitions between the disjointed series of rooms that had previously been divided and shut off from one another via traditional doors. The architect believed that opening up the apartment and redefining the navigation of its spaces would make it more inviting and livable. He proposed gutting the interior as much as the parameters of the building layout would allow (most of the walls were structural and couldn't be altered). Once that was done, Lynch went to work on a substantial eight-month surface renovation that added functional and aesthetic elements to transform the space from cramped and boxlike to spacious and sleek. Where doors and walls once stood, frosted translucent glass panels set into custom steel frames now delineate areas of differing function and purpose without chopping up the floor plan. "When closed, the glass panels convey ambient light to an interior that would have been artificially lit," Lynch points out. "Perceptually, light makes

The apartment is located on the thirtieth floor of a sixty-story high-rise in downtown Chicago (second building to the right).

Chicago High-Rise

Floor Plan

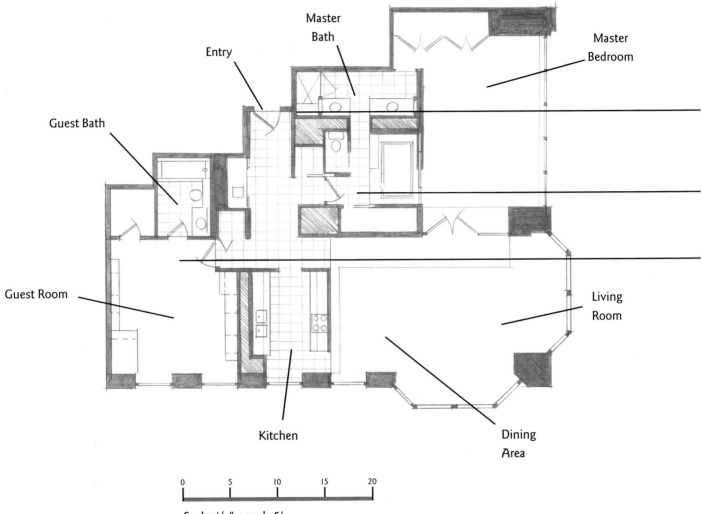

Entry

Master Bath

Master Bedroom

Guest Bath

Guest Room

Kitchen

Living Room

Dining Area

0   5   10   15   20

Scale: $^{1}/_{2}$" equals 5'

Sections

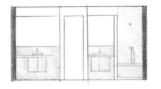

Section through Bathroom toward Living Room

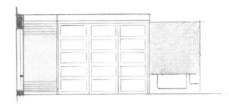

Section through Bedroom and Bathroom toward Living Room

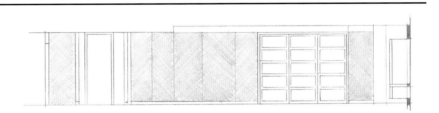

Section through Entry, Dining Area, and Living Room

High-Rise Apartment at Chicago, Illinois

1,600 Square Feet

Architect: Brad Lynch, Brininstool + Lynch Architects

Previous page:

Frosted translucent glass panels set into a steel frame provide a light-infusing separation between the bedroom and the main living space. Two of the three panels swing open to merge the two rooms. The newly dropped ceiling section in the living/dining room serves two purposes: it hides the unsightly sprinkler system and provides an additional opportunity for recessed lighting.

Item of Interest:
The living room chairs are available from Donghia.

The apartment's primary design elements are visible here: glass panels set into a steel frame and anigre wood HVAC unit covers. A small home fares better when materials are limited; doing so tricks the eye into seeing more space than is actually there.

The HVAC units in the original apartment were contained in unattractive metal boxes. Now, clip-on coverings of anigre wood and custom metal grillwork hide the units and also continue the apartment's materials theme.

relatively small spaces appear larger, so this apartment seems bigger than it actually is."

To add dimensional variation and create a "sense of anticipation" upon entering the apartment, Lynch manipulated the entry's ceiling heights and coves. The front hall houses a dual-purpose closet and bar that features anigre wood paneling and a backlit sliding pocket door made of frosted translucent glass set into a steel frame. Lynch also knew that smaller living spaces benefit greatly from consistency in detailing, or what he describes as "singular flavor"—in other words, too many design elements can compete with each other and detract

A wall and a narrow opening provide a simple unobstructed transition between the dining area and the kitchen, which is located on the other side of the wall. Anigre wood paneling adds warmth and a gentle hue to the room.

Items of Interest:
The dining set, console, and coffee table are original designs by:

Michael Heltzer
Heltzer Incorporated
4130 Rockwell Street
Chicago, IL 60618
(877) 561-5612 toll-free
www.heltzer.com

Save for minor changes, such as the addition of a stainless-steel back panel and new cabinet hardware, the small kitchen was left in its original state. The apartment's owner dines out frequently, so a large well-equipped kitchen was unnecessary.

from the space, overwhelming it visually and making it appear smaller than it is. This problem can be solved both with artistic restraint and by limiting the number of materials. Here, two materials—anigre wood and frosted glass—accomplish that goal with flair. Says Lynch of this design tactic, "The wood travels through the space, and this kind of consistency in detailing helps people orient and also see how the apartment is organized."

Minimizing distractions and moving toward a smoothness of design was also on Lynch's list of priorities. Before the remodel, the apartment's sprinkler system was visible in the ceiling of the living/dining

The owner, a collector of black-and-white photography and other art from around the world, wanted a clean backdrop for his treasures. The spare quality of the apartment, with its white walls and use of simple, straightforward materials, provides a museum-like setting for the display of special possessions.

room area. Lynch lowered the ceiling, hid the system in the added space above it, and installed recessed lighting to add ambience. The apartment's HVAC units were "in-wall and clunky," Lynch says, so he tore them out and redesigned their casings, disguising them in units made of anigre wood and custom steel grilles, a measure that increased the element of millwork throughout the space.

While this renovation required little or no structural change, the situation with the bathroom was different. Liska wanted to expand it, namely so it would be able to fit a three-foot-deep stainless-steel soaking tub. Although the ability to expand was extremely limited, Lynch figured out a way to grow the bathroom without encroaching on the rest of the living space: he took the square footage originally occupied by a hallway, added a raised platform, and installed the tub there. To continue the glass-and-steel theme, he added a glass panel on one side of the tub; the panel slides open to reveal a stunning skyline view through the living room windows. The bathroom expansion is an example of how a simple reorganization of space can increase the overall functionality of any room.

Lynch believes the apartment works because it has been kept very simple. "People tend to want to break up space and have as many rooms as possible," he says. "Here, rather than a bunch of rooms, we kept it more open but gave those spaces more function. Design is design. It's another challenge to make it work."

Regarding his transition into a small living space, Liska recalls that it was, in fact, painless. "Your life becomes easier when you scale back," he says. "I really do believe that less is more, that if you haven't eaten it, worn it, or touched it in six months, you don't need it."

The bath area is divided from the toilet and shower, which can be closed off with a sliding pocket door. Two sinks are located behind the white wall, which serves double duty as a place to display a photograph from the owner's collection; the photo is illuminated with a cove light. The custom soaking tub sits on a platform, and the glass panel, which is set into a pocket in the wall, slides open to reveal views of the skyline. Absolute black granite counters give the room a minimal, modern look.

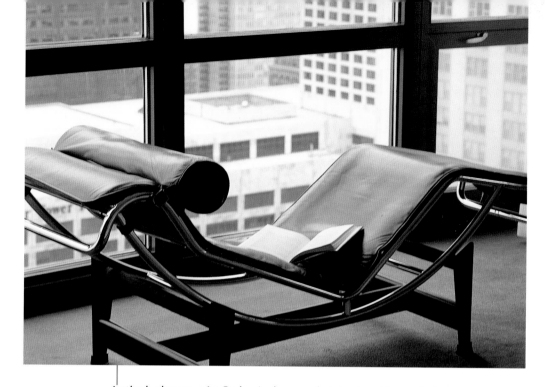

In the bedroom, a Le Corbusier lounge chair is placed for perfect views of the city. The window mullions have been painted the same color as the John Hancock Tower, which is visible from the apartment. Tying the windows to the exterior views in this manner creates a connection to the neighborhood—in this case, the heart of one of America's major cities. Because there is not a lot of furniture in the apartment, the eye is naturally directed toward the outside environment.

The master bedroom is a study in keeping a small space uncluttered and roomy. This was accomplished with generous storage, all of which is located behind a series of closet doors paneled in anigre wood, the apartment's signature material. The doors conceal multiple levels of storage, and the planes of the wood keep the space simple. The custom bed also features anigre wood.

Item of Interest:

The Le Corbusier chaise lounge is available from a variety of sources, including Design Within Reach (www.dwr.com) and Italian designer Casina.

5

A dilapidated shed is transformed into a master bedroom with exquisite scale and warm, inviting materials.

Something Old, Something New

Size: 520 square feet

Architect: Marla F. Croke Architecture, Inc.

Photographs: Gus Gusciora (interior) and Stephen Cieciuch (exterior)

Skylights bring light into the space and, in old buildings, are often easier to install than traditional windows. The north wall was closed off and turned into a storage bank; windows there would have reduced the bedroom's privacy, as neighbors are located right behind the building. The maple dresser fits perfectly into its specially designed niche, and the hallway was kept as narrow as possible to maximize the available space.

Sometimes, solutions can arise out of unexpected places. And, in some instances, a solution is so perfect it seems that none other would have been able to bring such a pleasing result.

This was the case with the Telluride, Colorado, home owned by Stephen Cieciuch (pronounced "chet-chu"), a real estate professional who moved to the former mining town in 1990. When he bought the circa-1892 house, its 1,200 square feet included two bedrooms and one bathroom. A separate two-story barn, erected behind the main house and used as a carpenter's workshop, held the potential for additional space, but Cieciuch wasn't sure how to incorporate it into the renovation. Instead, his main goal was to remodel the house, adding a second story for a master suite in the process. It was a workable solution but not perfect. Then his architect, Marla Croke of Telluride-based Marla F. Croke Architecture,

Inc., came up with a truly brilliant solution that took advantage of the space offered by the barn structure: Why not turn the barn into the master suite?

There was, however, a catch: Cieciuch didn't want the master suite to be in a separate building. To solve that problem, Croke came up with another great idea: link the house and the proposed master suite with a "connector"—an addition between the two buildings that would, as she puts it, "make it all into one house."

The renovation/addition plan worked for several key reasons: the town's architecture review board agreed that the new design did not interfere with the historic status of the house, it took advantage of the existing barn, and it conformed to the site's space restrictions without overwhelming it or the nearby neighbors. The house and the barn abut a steep and narrow alley, which meant there wasn't much room in which to expand. "Sometimes, a tight site is easier to work with," Croke notes, "because you have limited options."

Clad in rusted corrugated aluminum siding, the barn is architecturally distinct from the main house and, as Cieciuch says, "rustic and reminiscent of the mining era." Inside, this distinction was emphasized via various design elements, including exposed trusses of recycled old-growth Douglas fir timbers. Vertical-grain Douglas fir was used for the stairs leading up to the bedroom and for the shelves at the top of the landing, as well as for the closets, bathroom cabinets, and trim. The wood, combined with plaster-finish walls, exudes a feeling of warmth throughout the space. The flooring is old-growth wide-plank Ponderosa pine salvaged from the original barn.

The barn was in a state of severe disrepair before it was transformed into a master bedroom suite (with a garage and guest bedroom below) and attached to the main house. Here it is shown being lifted from its original location (there was no existing foundation—just wood framing and metal siding, for the most part) at the start of construction.

Telluride Addition

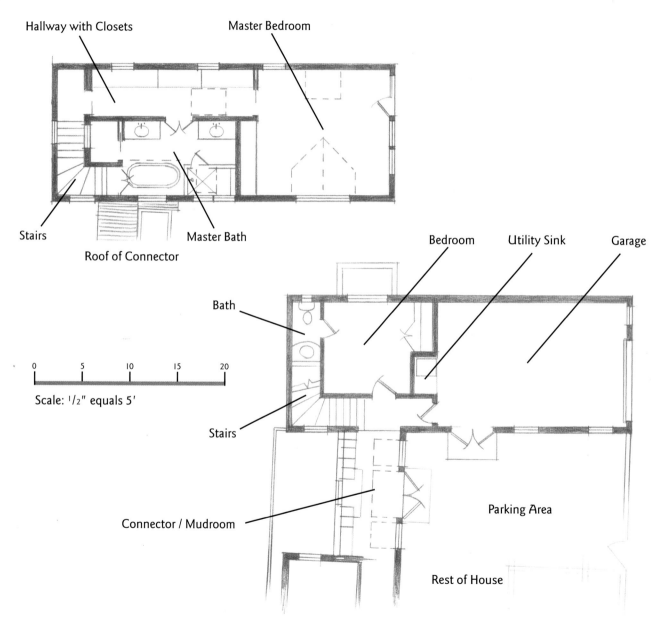

Hallway with Closets

Master Bedroom

Stairs

Roof of Connector

Master Bath

Bedroom

Utility Sink

Garage

Bath

0   5   10   15   20

Scale: $^{1}/_{2}$" equals 5'

Stairs

Connector / Mudroom

Parking Area

Rest of House

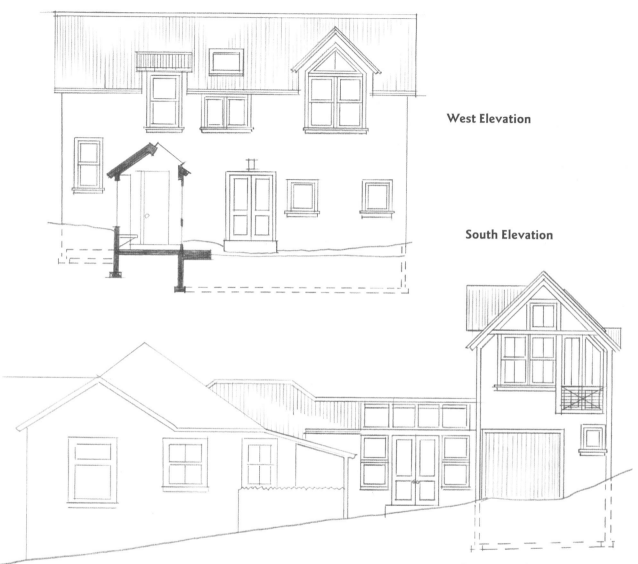

West Elevation

South Elevation

Barn Remodel at Telluride, Colorado

520 Square Feet

Architect: Marla F. Croke Architecture, Inc.

Painted poplar cubbyholes provide ample and accessible storage, a maple bench makes it easy to put on or take off shoes, and stone floors are durable enough to withstand the rigors of mountain living. Generously sized skylights and windows take the connector beyond its function as a mudroom/storage area by adding a sense of transparency and openness to the space. Also shown is the small extra bedroom, which is located within the original barn form, as is the garage.

Seen from the street, the main house and the barn behind it reveal how differing architectural styles can be successfully joined, and also how a space-restrictive site can be used to its fullest advantage.

The overall remodel and construction of the connector took fifteen months. The result is a study in scale, careful use of limited space, and keen attention paid to matters of privacy and practicality. Unlike some master suites with excessive square footage, towering cathedral ceilings, and enormous closets, this 520-square-foot space, while not exactly miniscule, is extremely livable. It is roomy but not palatial. Its ceiling is vaulted but not stratospheric. Many architects will attest to the appeal of a bedroom that doesn't feel cavernous and cold. Bedrooms, it has been said, should be designed to foster restful sleep and an atmosphere of reflection and retreat. Architecturally, this translates into lower ceilings, windows placed for light and also for privacy, materials that soften the space, and generous but unobtrusive storage. This master bedroom, with its accompanying his-and-hers bathroom, scores an A+ for scale. In addition to its "human" size, the materials enhance its inviting nature. The gentle calming tones of Douglas fir impart an eye-pleasing glow to the space, as do the frosted glass panels in the closet doors.

Because small spaces are prone to clutter unless belongings are either kept to a bare minimum or hidden away, Croke decided not to specify open closets or shelves except for the few built-ins on the north wall. The folding closet doors help keep the space streamlined. Beyond its simple beauty, the frosted glass in those doors serves another purpose: it hides the contents of the closet, keeping the space elegantly spare

Because the house is located so close to its neighbors, maintaining privacy was crucial. Window shades that raise from the bottom offer privacy without obstructing the stunning mountain views, and skylights bring in natural light. The exposed Douglas fir trusses are structural as well as aesthetically pleasing and impart architectural style to the space by visually drawing down the vaulted ceiling and keeping the scale of the room intimate. A king-size bed fits nicely into the bedroom without overwhelming it. Here, as in most small spaces that work well, the bedroom is comfortable but has no extraneous or wasted space.

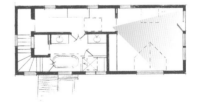

Items of Interest:
The walnut/maple/purple heart rocking chair and the maple dresser are original designs by:

Deep Creek Studio Fine Furniture
P.O. Box 3175
Telluride, CO 81435
(970) 626-5063
email:rich.projectworks@independence.net

Stairways and other key circulation areas in small houses should be kept as tight as possible so they don't take room away from living space. These stairs are tucked into the west end of the house. Built-in shelves in the landing wall offer both architectural relief to the end of the hallway and a tidy way to display photos and possessions. Wall sconces that light both up and down are functional and, because they are small, add to rather than detract from the space.

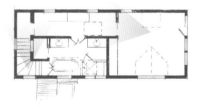

without restricting the materials to wood only—a fitting example of a successful merger between utility and aesthetics. Another space-conscious move involved the maple dresser unit that Cieciuch had purchased before the remodel. Rather than build the space first and think about how furniture would fit into it later, Cieciuch asked Croke to create a bedroom wall whose dimensions could accommodate the dresser, giving it the appearance of a built-in.

Combining a bedroom with a bathroom can be a tricky endeavor, particularly when it comes to allotting square footage for each. Sometimes the bathroom gets the short end of the stick. Cieciuch knew he didn't want to feel cramped; as a result the master space was essentially divided in half. To enhance light flow and create a sense of connection throughout the room, Croke suggested three-quarter-high bathroom walls; in fact, the only enclosed space in the master is the toilet, which can be closed off with a pocket door.

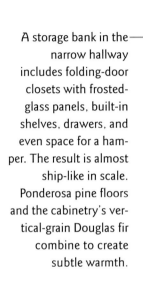

A storage bank in the narrow hallway includes folding-door closets with frosted-glass panels, built-in shelves, drawers, and even space for a hamper. The result is almost ship-like in scale. Ponderosa pine floors and the cabinetry's vertical-grain Douglas fir combine to create subtle warmth.

The connector serves as more than just a bridge between the main house and the master. For one, its construction allowed for a small extra bedroom beneath the master. It also is a highly functional addition to the home, namely because it serves as a mudroom, an essential part of any mountain dwelling. And, it provides plenty of convenient storage, with its wall of built-in shelves constructed of painted poplar. The built-ins bracket a maple bench and include two rows of coatracks. Stone, which is tough enough to withstand the rugged climate (and, thus, the rugged and often wet or muddy shoes) of the region, was selected for the floor.

Most significantly, the connector announces the separation between the master and the main house even as it fosters a sense of continuity throughout the entire property. Says Cieciuch, "When guests are staying over, they feel they have the whole house to themselves. It's very comfortable for people."

Three-quarter-high walls provide separation without closing off the space. This design tactic is especially important in smaller spaces, where too many floor-to-ceiling divisions can result in a cramped floor plan. The limestone sink countertop lends a bright contrast to the richness of the wood and adds another textural element to the room.

A modern steam shower with limestone accents shares space with a refurbished antique claw-foot tub, which was found in the original house. Roll-up window shades offer privacy without blocking the views.

The bedroom's exposed truss system is evident throughout the entire space, and three-quarter-high walls enhance the openness of the floor plan while at the same time providing some separation between functions. Small inlaid tiles around the towel racks add a touch of color to the room.

The bedroom is essentially one vaulted space divided by seven-foot-high walls that separate the bedroom from the bathroom and the bathroom from the hallway but don't close them off from one another. Due to space restrictions, the hallway became the bedroom's primary storage area.

The finished barn now serves a dual purpose as a master bedroom (upper level) and a garage and small guest bedroom (lower level). Its exterior pays homage to the town's mining heritage.

*An adventure in geometry
and a bold approach to
design turn a small addition
into a showstopper.*

A Fresh Angle

Size: 240 square feet

Architect: John Mike Cohen,
Cohen Hilberry Architects

Photographs: Sam Mitchell

It HALTS TRAFFIC on a regular basis and has even caused a few fender benders. One passerby went so far as to jot a note and leave it at the door: "Your home makes me grin—thanks for your humor," the anonymous writer said.

Described by some as the "Wizard of Oz" addition, this 240-square-foot studio office in Oakland, Missouri, near St. Louis, has plenty of people talking. Even the local newspaper ran a story on it. Beyond its curbside appeal, though, the studio announces—with head-turning surprise—that an addition to a traditional home doesn't have to adhere to an established style and can, in fact, do just the opposite with great success.

This "tweaked box," which is accessed off the front entry of the house, says plenty about the playful personalities of the individuals behind it: owner

The addition, clad in faux brick veneer applied to wood, was painted to match the house so that both seem to rise out of the rolling yard. The veneer simulates real brick but is less expensive. From an architectural standpoint, the house and the addition are miles away when viewed as individual units, but together they create a home that successfully combines traditional and contemporary design.

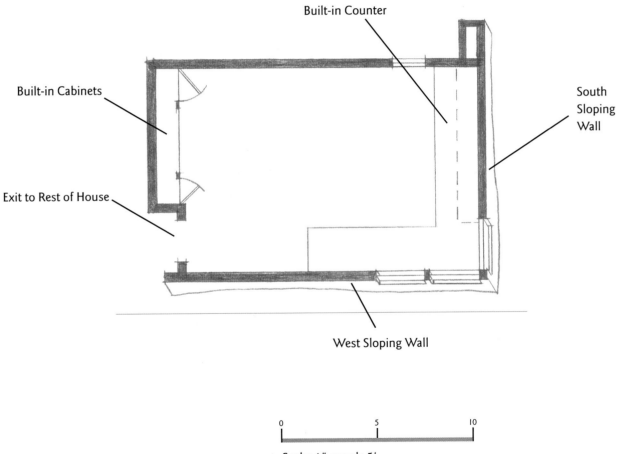

Built-in Counter

Built-in Cabinets

South Sloping Wall

Exit to Rest of House

West Sloping Wall

0　　　　　5　　　　　10

Scale: 1" equals 5'

South Elevation

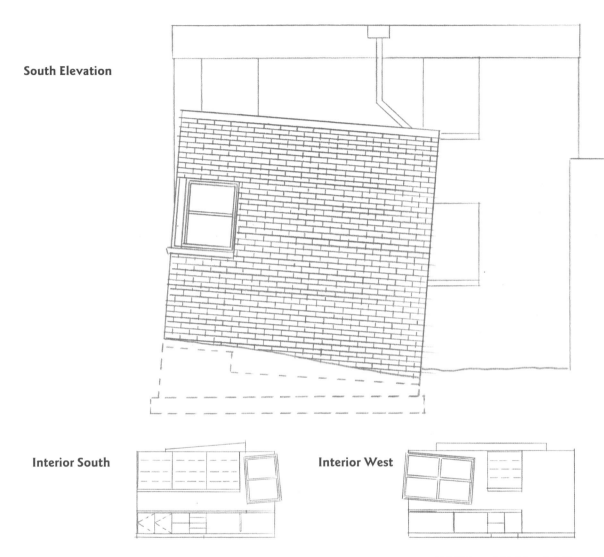

Interior South

Interior West

Addition at Oakland, Missouri

240 Square Feet

Architect: John Mike Cohen, Cohen Hilberry Architects

Sam Mitchell and architect John Mike Cohen. Longtime friends, the two collaborated on creating an adjoining office that would extend beyond its primary purpose—the goal was also to challenge ideas about what is considered to be visually correct. Explains Mitchell, who operates his photography business out of the studio, "I'm fascinated by how we as humans derive our perceptions. Who's to say what's right or wrong, what's normal or abnormal? Spending time in this space causes me to think about those concepts on a daily basis. Every time I look out the window, I have to rethink the way I perceive what's around me."

It's true that orthodox beliefs about spatial relationships must be tossed out of the (slanted) window when it comes to this piece of architectural fancy. With walls that are both tilted and rotated at five degrees, the addition stands out like the unruly child of its more conventional parent—a straightforward Art Deco—style home built in 1939 with nary a crooked line in

Great care was taken in joining the addition to the main house. The visible intersection between the two buildings became an integral part of the design, as revealed at the home's front entry. The addition penetrates the brick surface of the original house so that the two forms appear to slice into each other.

Oak floors and birch veneer cabinets and bookshelves, stained to match the floors, complement each other, and a melamine desktop provides a functional and practical surface. Keeping work-related materials stored behind cabinet doors keeps the small space uncluttered and maximizes the square footage. The two custom-made ottomans are also crafted of birch veneer to match the cabinets.

sight. Notes Mitchell, "Five degrees seems like a small amount, but it turns out to be a rather large number when you see it."

Not content just to place the addition's walls at atypical angles, the architect specified that they be thicker at the bottom than at the top to emphasize the tilting nature of the room. Although this move sacrificed some square footage inside, as the interior walls are not pitched and thus had to compensate for the exaggerated exterior measurements, both Cohen and Mitchell agreed that the result—an enhancement of the overall effect—was worth it. The final touch was a sloping roof to continue the theme of askew dimensionality. Attaching the addition to the house required thought, as well. Cohen wanted the two structures to trick the eye by simultaneously merging and standing apart from each other. To achieve this, he played up the angle of intersection, making it a prominent feature of the design. The new addition wall intersects the existing house wall seamlessly, thanks in part to the diligence of the builders, who chipped away at the bricks of the main house to create notches into which the addition could slide. "This intersection is really the key to the entire project," Mitchell points out. "Otherwise, it would just look like a box standing there—the intersection had to be perfect."

The initial plan for the addition involved placing it on the roof of the house as a second story. After studying the site, Cohen and Mitchell agreed that a more eco-nomical approach would be to build it in the side yard. Doing so gave the addition a deeper connection to its site: the undulations of the landscaped yard make the addition appear as if it is shooting out of the ground.

Aside from its striking geometry, the wood-frame addition is in essence a simple form, covered in faux brick veneer painted to match the main residence. Inside, a desk and cabinets share the space comfortably with a sleeper couch. Practical materials such as almond-colored melamine counters, birch veneer cabinets and oak floors complete the interior scheme and complement each other. Built-in glass shelves display the owner's special objects, which include chunks of iron sulfide crystals that grow naturally into spectacular configurations of perfect cubes—his inspiration for the addition.

"From any field of vision inside the studio, you can catch a glimpse of the motif," Cohen says. "In this way, the project was theater, but it was theater in the best sense because it makes such a strong statement—it was intended to shock. Still, theater should never overtake function, and we believe we accomplished this."

"With architecture," Mitchell adds, "people think it has to fit in a certain way, but it doesn't have to be like that. I recommend this to anyone: Take a shot at doing something fun."

Elegant recessed lighting used throughout the space illuminates the room without the requirement of standard lamps.

A birch veneer cabinet, which features built-in glass shelves for displaying belongings, also holds a small guest closet. The addition is accessed via a short hallway that follows from the main entry.

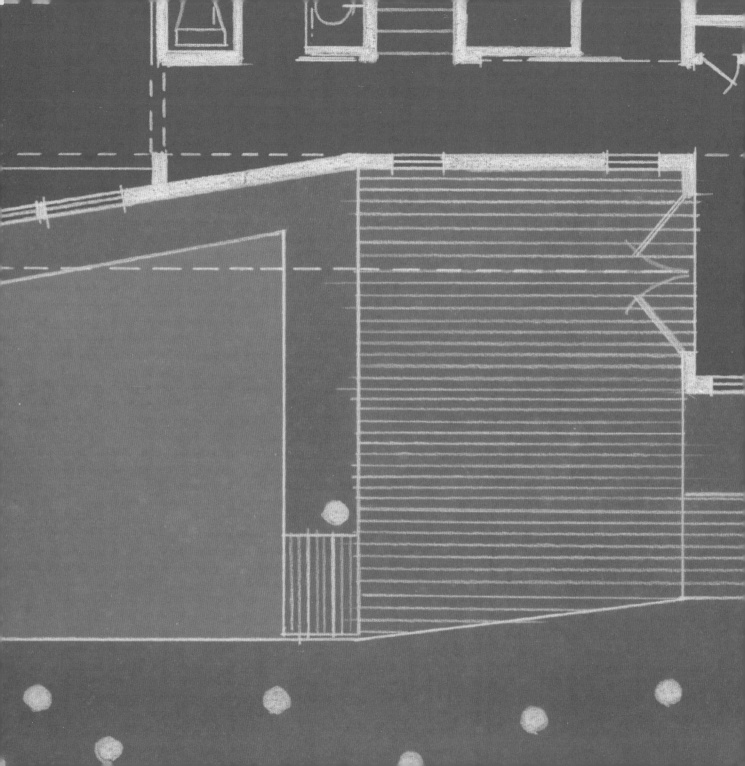

7

How one architect met the dual challenges
of an unusual site and a tight budget.

Trailer Park Living
with a Twist

Size: 2,400 square feet

Architect: Scott Lindenau, Studio B Architects

Photographs: Wayne Thom

House sketch: Scott Lindenau

The home's exterior responds to its environment with simple detailing and color that together create a vibrant and contemporary façade. Fasteners and joint connections have been left exposed, and exterior elements include simple and affordable materials such as corrugated Plexiglas, concrete panelboard, asphalt roofing paper, concrete masonry blocks, and corrugated tin.

ASPEN, COLORADO, RESIDENT and architect Scott Lindenau faced an increasingly common dilemma experienced by many who live in resort areas where the only consistent thing about the real estate market is that the prices keep rising.

Although owning a home in Aspen seemed beyond his financial reach, Lindenau, who graduated from the Rhode Island School of Design and then moved to the ski resort in 1986, didn't want to pack up and leave. At the same time, however, he understood he might never be able to afford a free-market house there, given that the average price of such a property now hovers in the seven digits. His innovative and cost-efficient solution? Build a single-family home in a trailer park.

A trailer park? Yes—but what Lindenau accomplished will cause even the most discriminating to retire any preconceived beliefs about trailer parks as places devoid of architectural grace and style. In Aspen, where land is at a premium, a trailer park makes very good sense.

Lindenau and his wife, Beyron, did hold a significant asset: they owned the 60 x 14-foot double-wide mobile home and the land on which it sat in Aspen's Smuggler Trailer Park. While it was an affordable existence, it wasn't exactly pleasant. "In the winter, the pipes would break and we had to wear scarves, hats, and gloves just to sit and watch a movie," the architect recalls. "And, there was no storage."

The couple endured eight drafty, cold, and generally uncomfortable years in the flimsy structure until they decided to sell the trailer and embark on the construction of a comfortable, design-conscious, affordable home that would

Local design guidelines mandated that the structure be no higher than thirteen feet. By incorporating the shed roof into the design, as well as exposed web trusses and walls that stop short of the ceiling, the result is an atmosphere of comfort and spaciousness. Sloping the ceiling's structure greatly increased the psychological "roominess" of the interiors, and natural light and views were enhanced via the use of the shed volume, making the form of the home critical to the success of the design. (See Sections.)

Aspen Hybrid

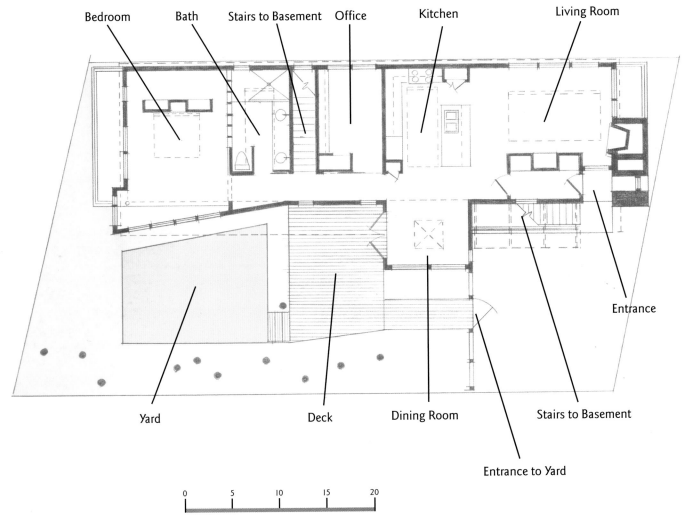

Bedroom   Bath   Stairs to Basement   Office   Kitchen   Living Room

Entrance

Yard   Deck   Dining Room   Stairs to Basement

Entrance to Yard

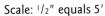

0   5   10   15   20

Scale: $^1/_2$" equals 5'

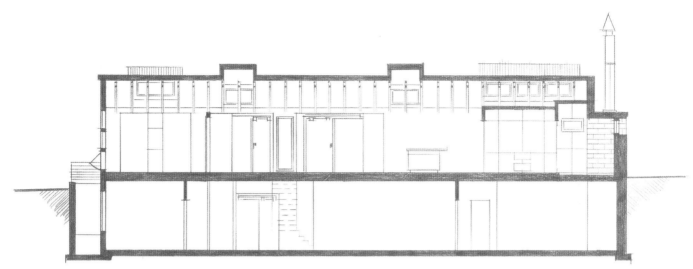

Section Looking North

**Section at
Living Room
Looking East**

**Section at
Kitchen / Dining Room
Looking East**

**Section at
Bedroom
Looking East**

Trailer Park Hybrid at Aspen, Colorado

2,400 Square Feet

Architect: Scott Lindenau, Studio B Architects

incorporate inexpensive and readily available materials and be able to accommodate their growing family.

The first challenge was the location itself: the narrow trailer lot is only 70 x 40 feet, which translates into approximately one-tenth of an acre. At 2,400 square feet, this home, affectionately known as the "Longhouse," is not small by some standards. However, its smallness is genuine because it has successfully adapted to the

124

realities of the land beneath it and the other homes around it. The house also provides one solution to Aspen's tight employee housing market: The Lindenaus and their two children live in 1,900 square feet of the house and rent a lower-level bedroom to one of Lindenau's employees.

The house, described by the architect as a "transformed trailer hybrid," was completed in six months at a cost of approximately $135 per square foot. Lindenau was able to save money by doing his own materials research and performing some of the general contracting. In many ways, the home is defined by what Lindenau chose not to cover up. For example, exposed fasteners, seams, patterns, and edges

Scott Lindenau, son Boris, and family dog Ruby watch as the original trailer leaves 320 Oak Lane. (Photo by Beyron Lindenau.)

Polished concrete floors and counters, maple plywood paneling, painted drywall, and exposed plywood ceilings with open-webbed joists comprise the home's interior palette. The design focuses on an open feel that still allows each room to be separate, which is important for a family. A variety of ceiling heights facilitates this effect; the ceilings change throughout the home as they define each space. Clerestory windows positioned high above the main living space bring in additional natural light and create a sense of spaciousness. Built-ins, shown in the living room, are a space-saving alternative to traditional cabinet storage.

Items of Interest:

The leather seating in the living room is by Ligne Roset. The bar stools at the kitchen counter are from IKEA.

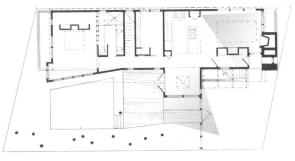

The narrow utilitarian hallway acts as a bridge between the home's public and private areas. Polished concrete floors are both practical (easily cleaned, they are popular with families with young children and pets) and affordable. Maple sliding doors impart simplicity and clean design.

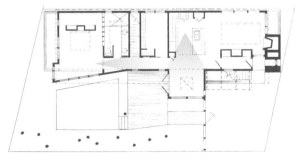

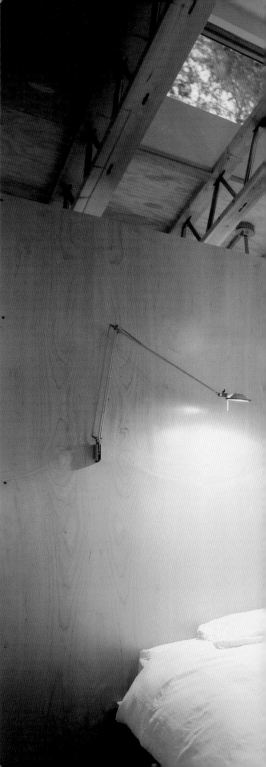

reveal what the architect calls "honesty in detailing, structure, and materials." In other words, the materials are not disguised by extraneous and perhaps unnecessary design embellishments and costly finish techniques, which can inflate a budget and at the same time have little direct effect on a home's livability. Keeping the bottom line firmly in mind, Lindenau chose standard lumberyard fare and then used the materials in "non-familiar" applications. To illustrate, inexpensive plastic, instead of the more expensive granite, tile, or wood, was fashioned into backsplashes for the kitchen and bathroom sinks. The maple-veneer plywood-

The master bedroom doubles as a home office along the east interior wall (not shown). The open feel of the design is continued with a "bed-wall" constructed of maple paneling that serves as a master walk-around closet on the opposite side of the bed, a clever storage technique. Sanded Plexiglas panels form the wall and disperse natural light, while maple sliding doors furnished with brushed-aluminum hardware provide an economical, stylish, and space-conscious way to close off the room. Built-ins above the bed are a clutter-free and streamlined way to add storage, and the reading lamps attached to the wall enhance comfort and eliminate the need for bedside tables.

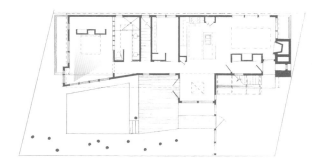

panel walls in the house are significantly less expensive than plaster-finish walls, for example, and the plywood's hue lends subtle warmth to the interior without the requirement of paint. Other budget-friendly materials include Plexiglas walls, concrete counters and floors, standard structural ceiling trusses, cinder block, exterior plank siding, and corrugated tin walls (exterior).

Lindenau employed another clever architectural technique to save money: he stopped the walls short of the ceiling, which has the added benefit of encouraging the transmittal of natural light throughout the home and enhancing air circulation. Because the house sits so close to its neighbors, privacy was a key issue, and Lindenau met that particular challenge with strategically placed windows, most notably the clerestory windows in the main living areas. Another privacy measure: a basic cinder-block wall punctuated with a few tiny windows serves as the home's façade; the larger windows and key design elements were saved for the sides and back of the house, where maintaining privacy was not as crucial.

By all accounts, this unusually sited and design-savvy house has been a successful lifestyle transition for this young family. As Lindenau sums it up, "When you're in the house, you can't even tell you're in a trailer park."

Lindenau used common materials in unconventional ways. Here, concrete for floors and countertops, as well as sandblasted Plexiglas and maple plywood paneling for interior walls and ceilings, separate the master bathroom from the rest of the house, maintaining the simplicity of the home's design.

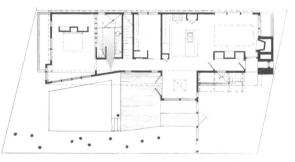

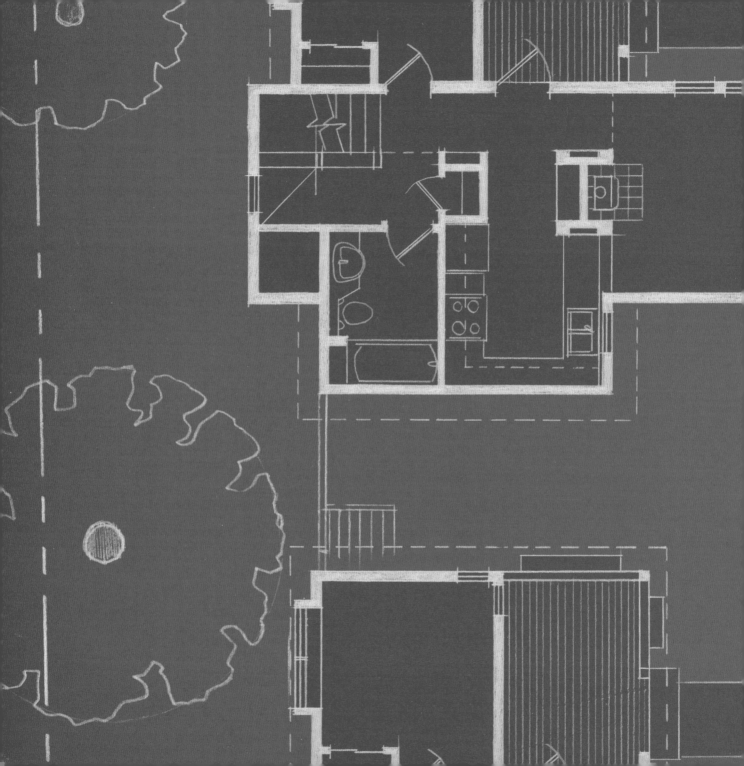

8

*A cluster of tiny cottages
offers gracious scaled–back
living and an opportunity to
join a community.*

A Neighborly Development

Size: All under 1,000 square feet

Architects: Ross Chapin, John Prietto,
Eric Richmond, Matthew Swett,
Ross Chapin Architects

Developer: Jim Soules, The Cottage Company

Photographs: Ross Chapin

The neighborhood's grid follows the concept of "layering," which forms understated separations between the cottages and keeps them within the context of their overall setting. Such delineations include a front gate entry into the neighborhood, walkways that border the central commons, strategically placed flowerbeds, and small fences and gates that mark the boundaries of the homes without closing them off from each other.

WITH THEIR QUAINT APPEARANCE, colorful landscaped gardens, and placement around a shared lawn, the Greenwood Avenue Cottages seem to have emerged from a bygone era when housing developments were designed with the premise that they should be places where people gather to establish a sense of community.

Located in Shoreline, Washington, a town near Seattle that has adopted its own cottage-housing development code, the Greenwood project is the fourth such "pocket neighborhood" by The Cottage Company, a development firm that has received widespread kudos for its thoughtful and visionary approach to modern housing. Basing its guiding principles on the belief that a growing number of individuals are attracted to a simpler, richer lifestyle in the context of a neighborhood, The Cottage Company has finessed a formula for success: build beautifully scaled, well-crafted, livable homes in a refreshingly out-of-the-ordinary milieu. Homebuyers have embraced this philosophy: the Greenwood homes enjoyed brisk sales as soon as they reached the market.

The Cottage Company is the brainchild of architect Ross Chapin and builder/developer Jim Soules, who have long held that people will be receptive to imaginative and sensible ideas about shelter if they can see and touch the real thing. In a time when suburban sprawl threatens to consume thousands of acres of land and further crowd already stressed highways, a mind-set is beginning to emerge—that life can follow the concept of proximity to neighbors and also to key services such as shopping and schools. The Greenwood Avenue Cottages and other such Cottage Company developments have been the solution for those who appreciate the benefits of living in clustered homes arranged to ensure that privacy is not compromised.

"These 'right-sized' houses are in response to our frustration with land being chewed up by endless acres of huge houses," explains Ross Chapin. "Most developments are manicured streets of garage doors where people are sequestered to their backyards with high fences. There is little opportunity for neighbors to meet and know one another. Houses are designed for resale rather than real needs. Yet, we have found

The cottages have been painted in a variety of colors, but each is trimmed in white to tie the homes together and extend a sense of continuity throughout the neighborhood.

Shoreline Cottages

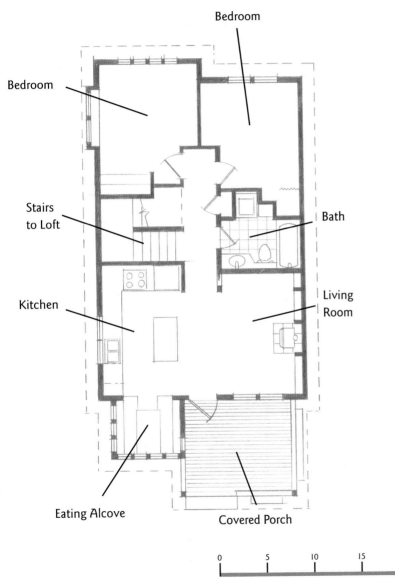

Bedroom

Bedroom

Stairs
to Loft

Kitchen

Bath

Living
Room

Eating Alcove

Covered Porch

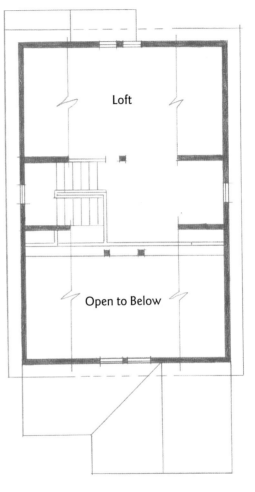

Loft

Open to Below

Plan "A"

0   5   10   15   20

Scale: $1/2$" equals 5'

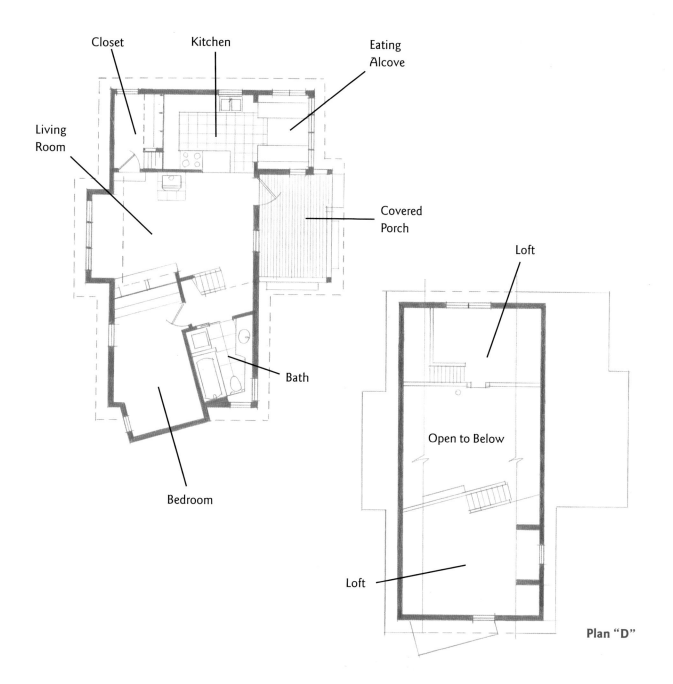

Closet

Kitchen

Eating
Alcove

Living
Room

Covered
Porch

Loft

Bath

Open to Below

Loft

Bedroom

Plan "D"

143

Shoreline Cottages

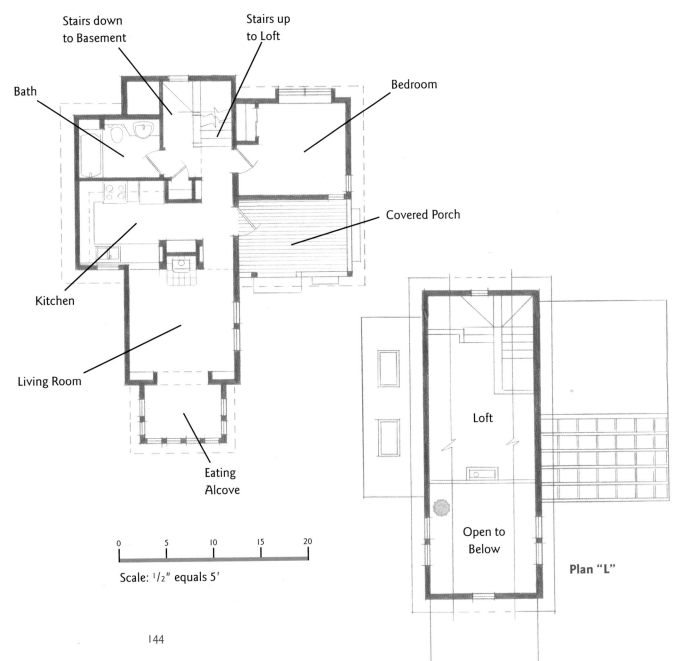

Stairs down to Basement

Stairs up to Loft

Bath

Bedroom

Kitchen

Covered Porch

Living Room

Eating Alcove

0   5   10   15   20

Scale: $^1/_2''$ equals 5'

Loft

Open to Below

Plan "L"

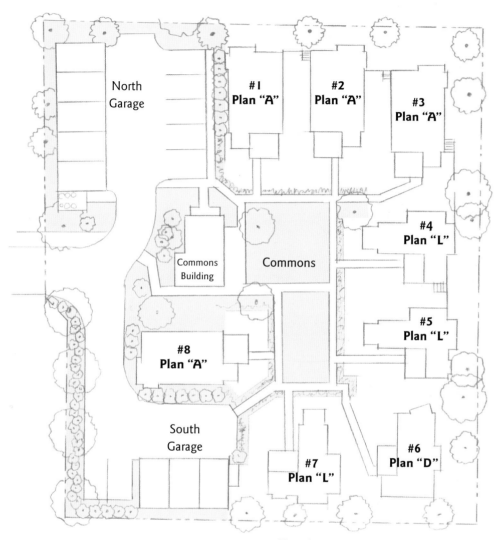

North
Garage

#1
Plan "A"

#2
Plan "A"

#3
Plan "A"

#4
Plan "L"

Commons
Building

Commons

#5
Plan "L"

#8
Plan "A"

South
Garage

#7
Plan "L"

#6
Plan "D"

Housing Community at Shoreline, Washington

All under 1,000 Square Feet

Architects: Ross Chapin, John Prietto, Eric Richmond, Matthew Swett,
Ross Chapin Architects

that there is a tremendous niche of people who want to have a simpler lifestyle tailored to how they actually live. Our goal is to create places that inspire a renaissance of vital neighborhoods and communities."

Each of the eight cottages has its own charming allure and carefully wrought details that appeal to the human need to nest. Under 1,000 square feet in size and offered in three different floor plans, the homes have one-and-a-half stories that can accommodate one or two bedrooms and a usable loft as well as a comfortable kitchen/dining area. Their spaciousness belies their compact dimensions, thanks to floor plans that pay attention to key elements such as positioning of windows and skylights, diagonal views, framed openings, and a variety of ceiling heights. Interior materials include wood floors and walls, energy-efficient windows, and gas stove-type fireplaces. Each cottage has a private backyard and is fronted by a porch that serves as a transition between the home and the commons. Says Chapin, "The porch is one of the key elements to fostering neighborliness. It's a safe place to engage with others on your own terms. For this reason, they are open rather than enclosed." Raised flower boxes contribute color and fragrance to the porch and are a way for each household to express itself. Greenwood also includes a community building, a parking garage set off to the side of the property, and a shared toolshed.

To forge a balance between the public and private, each cottage features a hierarchy of room placement that relates to function. For example, because they require more concealment, the bedrooms and bathroom are situated toward the back of the house, while the living room and kitchen—more open and public places—are at the front, which faces the lawn. Because the commons is visible from the houses, residents can easily see who is walking through it—and perhaps who should not be there. "It facilitates the idea of neighbors looking out for each other," Chapin points out.

This classic gable home has two bedrooms on the main level and a spacious loft. As with all the cottages, the more public aspects of the interior face the commons, a strategy that meets one of the goals behind the neighborhood concept: neighbors watching out for each other. The homeowners experience a greater level of comfort and security because they can readily see what is happening around them.

The features of this cottage floor plan reveal architectural tricks that make the house appear larger. For example, the interplay of different ceiling heights in the living room and adjacent dining nook offer visual variation, and high windows send natural light deep into the space. Built-ins are a tidy solution for storing personal objects.

The cozy dining area in this cottage is placed at the front of the house, where ample windows train the focus toward the commons area, thus forming a link between the inside and outside spaces. In this floor plan, a full dining table fits perfectly into a light-filled corner of the kitchen.

Indeed, every aspect of the Greenwood site plan was carefully studied, from how people navigate the property to where the garage is located. Chapin describes this technique as a "layering," meant to guide residents through a series of experiences as they approach their homes. To illustrate, a person entering Greenwood walks through a main gate and is then directed into the commons via a paved pathway. Small handmade wooden fences and "implied" gates act as gentle separations between the commons and the homes;

This loft bedroom can accommodate twin beds and a compact storage unit and shelving. A skylight floods the loft with daylight.

The straightforward lines of the living room blend effortlessly with the loft situated above. Keeping materials bright and simple in small houses creates the illusion of more space, as is evident here in the home's elegant whitewashed pine loft detail and walls painted in luminous tones.

The low fences and gates are made of scrap-wood cuttings from a local lumber mill.

passing through a home's gate, then, represents an entrance into another layer. From there, the layering continues to the porch and then to the inside.

"This layering is so central and key to the success of this project," Chapin explains. "The low fences and gates that border the houses provide a psychological definition of separation, as they mark the edge of the owners' personal boundaries. This is important in closely set neighborhoods, where people still need to feel as though they have their own space around them."

To encourage a connection between public and private spaces and enhance community togetherness, the cottages look out onto a central commons and have open porches that encourage interaction between residents.

Although the houses are in close proximity, the design of the neighborhood allows residents to establish their own sense of space.

Overleaf:
The roomy porches were kept open to extend the livable space of the cottages and create the feeling of a more traditional neighborhood.

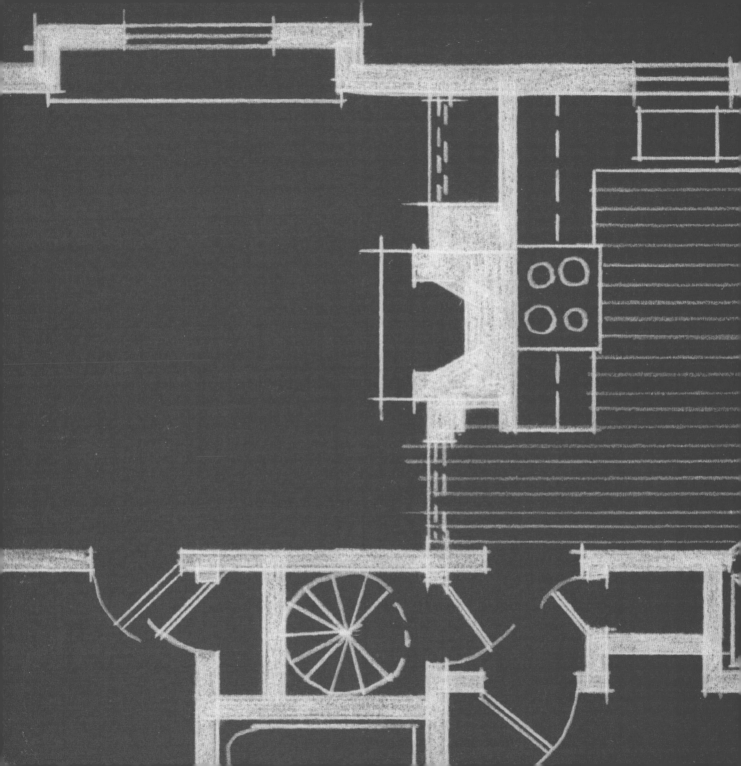

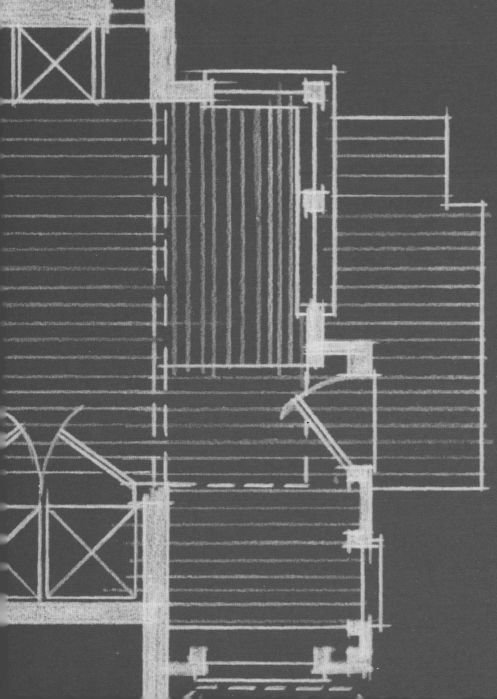

9

*How a Berkeley
bungalow went from
"everyday" to "wow!"
with a whimsical
light-filled addition
and the use of
unexpected
materials.*

A Small Addition
Makes a Big Difference

Size: 728 square feet

Architects: David Arkin and Anni Tilt,
Arkin Tilt Architects

Photographs: Edward Caldwell

Imagine that you could change the entire character of your home by adding just twenty-eight square feet. One vivid example of how this is possible is the Berkeley, California, bungalow owned by two professors of ecology and landscape architecture.

The 1920s-era house, originally 700 square feet and built in the Craftsman style, was cozy but cramped; the owners were beginning to feel hemmed in, particularly by the home's small, dark dine-in kitchen. Devoted environmentalists and proponents of both the living small philosophy and the green building movement, they hired David Arkin and Anni Tilt of Arkin Tilt Architects, whose reputation for environmentally conscious architecture appealed to their own sensibilities. The architects were asked to devise a solution that would liven up the house, create a

Berkeley Addition

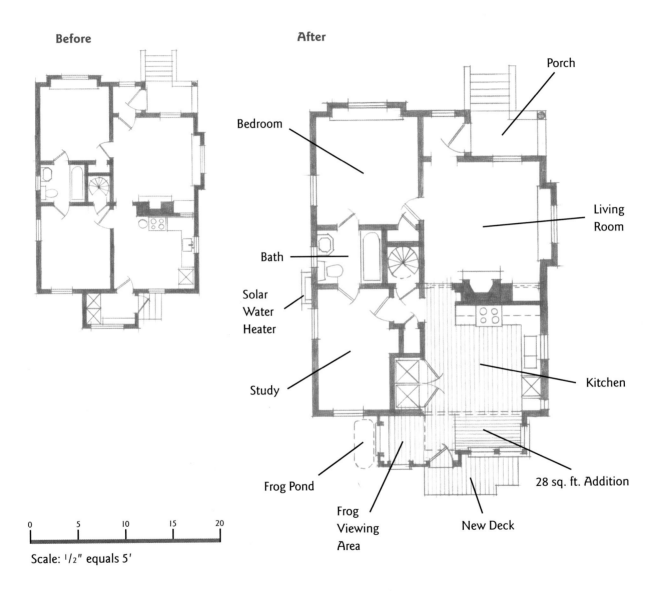

Before

After

Porch

Bedroom

Living Room

Bath

Solar Water Heater

Study

Kitchen

Frog Pond

Frog Viewing Area

New Deck

28 sq. ft. Addition

0   5   10   15   20

Scale: $^1/_2''$ equals 5'

Residence Addition at Berkeley, California

728 Square Feet

Architects: David Arkin and Anni Tilt,
Arkin Tilt Architects

stronger connection with the garden, use recycled materials and "zero-waste" construction techniques, and be affordable.

Arkin and Tilt responded with a clever design for a $55,000 remodel whose prominent features are a twenty-eight-square-foot addition to the garden-side kitchen and an overhaul of a former laundry room. "The northeast facing kitchen was abysmally dark," Tilt recalls. "Our challenge was to figure out how to expand it and bring in more light without impinging on the garden on the one side yet retaining the integrity of the living room on the other. It was crucial that we keep what worked well about the home as we updated it."

To open up the floor plan, the architects removed the back wall of the kitchen, leaving some of the original framing. Rather than use a new steel beam to span the opening, the architects and the contractor tracked down a well-preserved railroad track, circa 1880, at a train salvage yard in Stockton, California. "We are always on the lookout for ways to use interesting recycled and reused materials," Arkin says. Tilt adds, "And that begins with what's there. Revealing the old, fabulous framing shows off the 'bones' of the house while allowing light to move through the entire space."

The home's twenty-eight-square-foot addition has a curving roof made of corrugated metal with siding consisting of license plate "shingles." The red door opens into the kitchen and a laundry-area-turned-sitting-nook. The deck, made from redwood salvaged by the contractor, incorporates a special element: a bottom step made of a limestone fence post found in Kansas. Clerestory windows let sunlight into the adjacent kitchen. The boldly colored door and windows stand out from the dark wood siding, highlighting the home's new contemporary features.

The addition's curved roof sweeps up and over the former laundry shed. The shed was insulated on the exterior, then clad with rustic offcuts from a lumber-salvage company. The salvaged window was intentionally set low to foster an intimate look into the yard, keeping the focus oriented at ground level rather than toward a neighboring house.

By far the most striking aspect of the revamped home is the addition, whose exuberant curved metal roof rises over the existing roof like a wave. Beyond its undeniable visual interest, the curve also performs an important function: its soaring volume provides clerestory windows in the south-east corner, bringing much-needed ambient light into the house, especially when the sun is low in the sky during the winter months. Additional day-light flows in via a glass door and generous win-dow placement.

The addition exterior offers up a touch of practi-cal whimsy. Clad in hundreds of license plate "shingles" painstakingly gathered by the owners, it sits in bold contrast to the home's unassuming wood shingles. Arkin and Tilt explain that their original suggestion of flattened tin cans, as used by some early settlers in the high Sierras, was vetoed when a sample panel rusted out in a matter of weeks in the coastal humidity. Further brain-storming brought up the idea of license plates, which are already shingle-like in nature and come coated for weather resistance. The owners valiantly embarked on a license-plate-finding mission. All fifty states are represented by the plates, whose placement is anything but arbitrary—the owners spent hours arranging them to produce the exact pattern they wanted.

In another resourceful move, Arkin and Tilt transformed the south-facing laundry near the kitchen into a sitting nook that broadens the space and reveals intimate views of the garden. The architects worked with the existing bead board and framing on the interior, placing a salvaged window low on the south wall. "The window is positioned so that you don't see the neighbor—you look down into the garden instead," Tilt explains. "It has a delightfully intimate scale to it." This retreat-like corner of the house has been dubbed the "frog-viewing room" because it looks directly onto an old claw-foot bathtub that serves as a frog pond below.

Altogether, the addition is an adventurous stroke of color that manages to blend into its neighbor-hood. Says Tilt, "From the street, you'd never know there had been a renovation. It looks like a typical, rather nondescript bungalow, but you find something unexpected in the back."

Alterations in the paneled living space are more in keeping with the Craftsman-style interior. A new fireplace with a cast concrete surround has been placed where the old one stood, and operable transom windows between the kitchen and the liv-ing room brighten and renew the home while allowing it to retain its original charm.

The remodel also makes long-term economic sense: by providing ample daylighting, coupled with solar hot water, increased insulation, and a new refrigerator, the house is not only more liv-able, it also consumes half as much energy as it did before the modifications.

A salvaged railroad track now supports the original framing exposed to allow an unobstructed path to the addition. The unusual beam also acts as a transition between the kitchen and the addition. This transition is further articulated in the flooring: the floor at the addition is laminated bamboo, delineated with an exotic hardwood edge to distinguish it from the existing Douglas fir subflooring newly revealed under the old sheet vinyl.

Item of Interest:
The recycled glass countertops in the kitchen are available from:

Counter/Production
701 Bancroft Way
Berkeley, CA 94710
(510) 843-6916
www.counterproduction.com

The kitchen's basic layout was unchanged, but a hot water heater was relocated to the exterior and supplemented with a solar unit. The old refrigerator was replaced with a tall, narrow, energy-efficient model. Also visible is the railroad-tie beam that supports the end wall. Standard off-the-shelf cabinets are a money-saving option.

For Arkin and Tilt, the project revealed unconventional ways of approaching small spaces and enhancing their livability and fun factor. "One of our goals is to build as little as possible," Arkin says. "It's about quality versus quantity, and with this home, it's also about the joy of collaborating with owners and a contractor, all focused on a common goal of showcasing reused and recycled materials. The result is both playful and very personal."

To borrow light from the adjacent kitchen while preserving the home's Craftsman style, the architects placed transom windows above the living room's built-in cabinetry to the left and right of the rebuilt fireplace, styling it to match the original redwood casework. The transoms can be opened for air circulation. The cast-concrete fireplace surround is imprinted with oak and hickory leaves collected by the owner at his childhood home in North Carolina.

The kitchen countertop reveals the aesthetic potential of recycled materials. Here, salvaged tempered glass embedded with a smattering of the owners' personal items, such as marbles and jacks, forms the aggregate in a concrete-like counter, providing a durable, elegant, and environmentally friendly surface.

Item of Interest:

The cast concrete fireplace is by:

Sonoma Cast Stone
1741 Morningside Mountain Road
Glen Ellen, CA 95442
(888) 807-4234
www.sonomastone.com

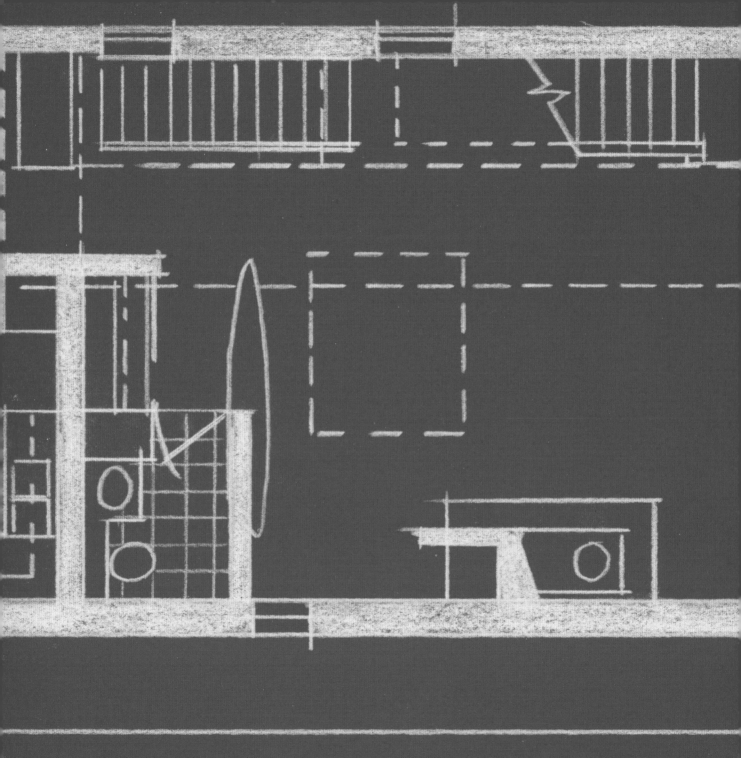

10

A home with a "split personality" blends into its neighborhood and offers a welcome glimpse of architectural surprise.

A Contemporary Slant
on a Traditional House

Size: 1,600 square feet

Architects: David Brininstool and Brad Lynch, Brininstool + Lynch Architects

Photographs: Jamie Padgett

Queen Anne–style homes are common in traditional Midwest neighborhoods such as this one, located west of Chicago's Wrigley Field.

FROM THE STREET, this small unassuming house on the north side of Chicago looks like a typical Queen Anne–style home, with its steep gable roof, bay windows, and modestly ornamented portico. When viewed from the back, however, the house's split personality is revealed in the form of an unexpectedly contemporary palette—a drastic make-over intended to give it a fresh, updated look without isolating it from its surroundings. The approach worked for the owner, who wanted to modernize the house but didn't want it to stand out unnaturally from its architecturally similar peers.

"When viewed from the north-side city street, the restored house offers context in agreement with the neighborhood," explains architect Brad Lynch. "The back of the house still has a gable roof, but the configuration of windows and materials creates a more modern interpretation. You can't tell what's going on inside or at the rear of the house by looking at it from the front."

While the house façade speaks to days gone by, the back reflects the contemporary inclination of the owner and also of Lynch, who along with David Brininstool was called upon to transform the dilapidated structure into a stylish, livable home—all on a frugal budget. In the end, the architects achieved their goal: the final remodeling costs came to about $65 per square foot in 1991.

Like many homes of the era, the house has what Lynch describes as a "shotgun" floor plan, characterized by a front-to-back arrangement of rooms in which the primary living section sits directly beyond the front entrance, with other areas following from there and the kitchen typically placed at the very back of the house. While sensible in its own way, this kind of plan tends to have a shrinking effect on already limited square footage. Adding to the challenge was the fact that at some point in its history, the house had been divided into three separate apartments.

To remedy these basic problems and develop a more graceful organization of space in which light and materials dominate rather than walls and corridors, the architects gutted the house, opening it up significantly and liberating the floor plan from its previous restraints. The result is one of fluidity. Gone are the old walls, replaced with a curved "floating" wall made of tinted plaster and structural steel, then coated with a clear wax to produce a rich sculptural quality. The floating wall makes a sophisticated statement about the possibilities of budget-conscious design, and it serves the key purpose of dividing areas of function without traditional walls. To illustrate, the living room wall was placed in front of a small hallway, which houses a guest closet and a powder room. The wall hides this more utilitarian part of the house from the seating area. A fluted glass panel and layered ceiling heights add to the home's expansive feeling.

The contemporary exterior at the back of the house was achieved through an updated reconfiguration of window style, size, and placement. Due to its tight location between two other structures, the home's width could not be increased to add more space. Instead, the architects focused on the inside of the house, gutting it and reworking the old-fashioned floor plan into one that is ultimately more livable and aesthetically pleasing.

Chicago Remodel

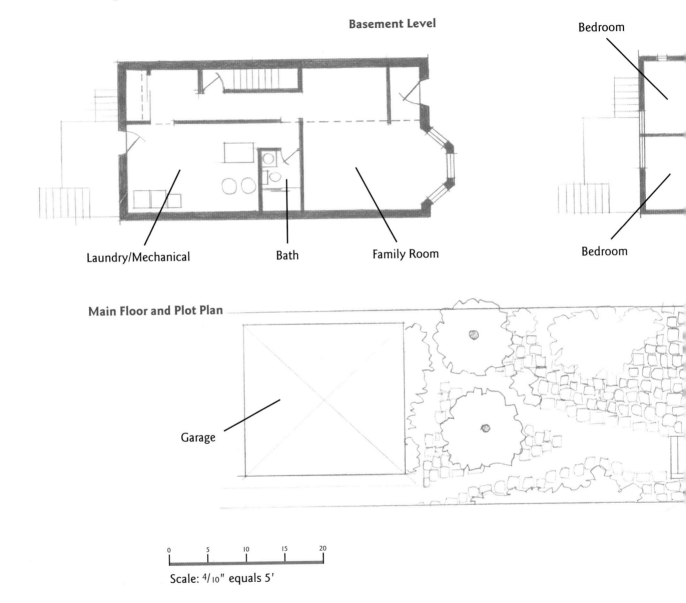

Basement Level

Laundry/Mechanical

Bath

Family Room

Bedroom

Bedroom

Main Floor and Plot Plan

Garage

0   5   10   15   20

Scale: 4/10" equals 5'

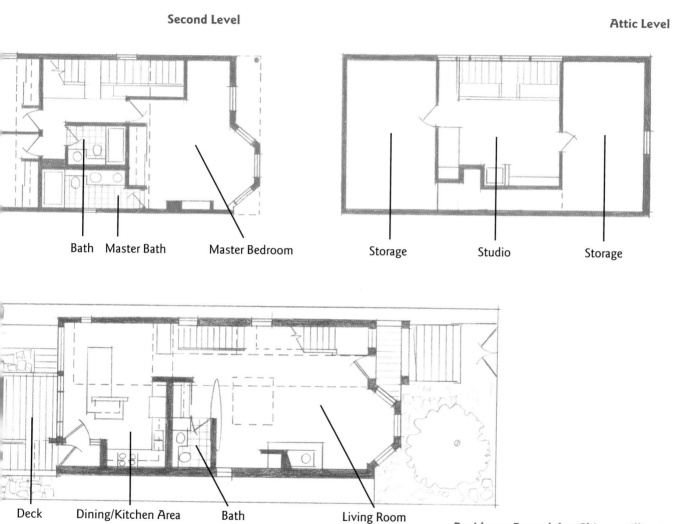

Second Level

Attic Level

Bath   Master Bath   Master Bedroom

Storage   Studio   Storage

Deck   Dining/Kitchen Area   Bath   Living Room

Residence Remodel at Chicago, Illinois

1,600 Square Feet

Architects: David Brininstool and Brad Lynch, Brininstool + Lynch Architects

The varying ceiling heights, in fact, ended up becoming one of the home's dominant design features. The architects were hindered somewhat by the spatial confines of the house—it is only twenty feet wide. To create the illusion of more depth and to add artistic variation, they played with planes of uneven ceiling heights, altering the formerly straightforward ceiling so that the rooms now breathe with engaging angles, an effect that is further enhanced through recessed cove lighting. Lynch believes that the three-dimensional appearance of the layered ceiling acts as an invitation into the heart of the space. "It fosters a sense of anticipation as you move toward the next area—you're invited back to see what's next in the house," he points out. To further build on this infusion of geometry, the walls and ceiling layers were painted in seven shades of white—from light to dark. This economical trick can do wonders for a small space.

Column supports are not typically given consideration as design elements, and more often than not they are hidden behind drywall. Brininstool and Lynch, however, decided to incorporate this necessary structural component right into the home's interior theme. The two steel-composite columns on the first floor are comprised of four unequal angles set against each other to form a quarter-inch reveal that imparts an unexpected pattern. "Rather than disguise the columns, we exposed them to make the space more interesting," Lynch explains. "The result is that the columns create a composition on their own."

Lynch believes the house provides an excellent example of living small. "Small is really about a better quality of space and editing the things you own so that you can retain that quality of space," he says.

Overleaf:

The stairway to the second floor is made of structural steel with solid oak treads, which continue the theme of the red oak floors present throughout the house. Translucent glass is affordable and durable and also performs the important function of facilitating light flow, which is critical in a small space in a densely platted neighborhood where windows must be placed primarily with privacy in mind.

To keep costs down, the architects retained the home's original exterior framing and restored and reused the basic roof. Thanks to these cost-saving measures, the remodel successfully adhered to the constraints of the owner's limited budget.

The home's entire first floor is now a beautifully unfettered space, as shown in this view from the front seating area back toward the kitchen/dining area. The living room's "floating" curved wall offers an elegant suggestion of where the living room ends and the kitchen begins. A light-filtering futex glass panel set into a steel frame acts as a support for the stairway railing leading to the basement. The glass panel meets the need for a railing support without necessitating a solid wall.

Layered ceiling heights have taken the space from ordinary to interesting. The furniture in the seating area was kept to a minimum; too many furnishings would have crowded the room, negating the architects' goal of instilling a sense of spaciousness within the confines of the small and narrow floor plan.

The compact kitchen/dining area features a built-in table made of green marble. To minimize obstructions to the backyard patio and garden views, visible through the home's generous windows, the tabletop is supported only by a thin steel column. A tinted-plaster wall similar to the one in the living room separates the kitchen from the dining nook, creating the illusion of individual cooking and eating areas. The cohesiveness of the area, however, is revealed in how the table continues on the kitchen side of the yellow wall. The column in the foreground is necessary, as it supports a second-floor beam, but its unusual construction—four unequal column angles—makes it as much of an artistic element as a structural one.

The home's attic was turned into an artist's studio, and it reveals the possibilities of a clean, uncluttered space. The attic is furnished minimally with simple materials, which makes it seem larger than it is. Red oak floors add natural color to the room and provide a warm contrast to the white walls and the spare shelving and work surfaces.

CHOOSING AN ARCHITECT is a highly personal process, and the best owner-architect relationship will combine aspects of synergy, design sensibility, and economic feasibility. Here are a few tips for selecting the right professional to help you create your small space:

→ Interview several architects before you plunge in (note that some architects charge fees for interviews).

→ Before you schedule meetings with architects, take the time to carefully review your design and construction budget so you can communicate both your dreams and your limits.

→ Ask the architectural firm in question for the names of past clients who would be willing to share their experiences.

→ Take the time to visit a home your architect has designed so you can get a better sense of the architect's approach.

How to Find an Architect

→ If you are restoring or renovating a home, ask your local zoning board for recommendations.

→ Research the architect's license, other professional credentials, and/or awards.

→ Educate yourself by learning basic architectural terms and techniques. For example, Francis D. K. Ching's *A Visual Dictionary of Architecture* is an excellent compendium of definitions and descriptions.

→ Consider hiring a project manager (also called an owner's representative). This professional represents your best interests in the design and building process, primarily by acting as an intermediary between you and the architect and builder. A project manager will monitor your budget, track construction progress, and generally help keep things running as smoothly as possible.

Organizations

American Institute of
Architects (AIA)

1735 New York Avenue NW

Washington, DC 20006

(800) AIA-3837

www.aia.org

www.aiaonline.com

National Association of Home
Builders Research Center

400 Prince George's Boulevard

Upper Marlboro, MD 20774

(800) 638-8556

www.nahbrc.org

American Institute of Building
Design

2505 Main Street, Ste 209B

Stratford, CT 06615

(800) 366-2423

www.aibd.org

Architecture Research Institute

119 East 35th Street

New York, NY 10016

(212) 725-7200

www.architect.org

Photographers

Ed Caldwell

Ed Caldwell Location
Photography

1783 – 29th Avenue

San Francisco, CA 94122

(415) 664-9873

ed@edwardcaldwell.com

www.edwardcaldwell.com

Gus Gusciora

G-Stop Photography

P.O. Box 630

Telluride, CO 81435-0630

(970) 728-0386

gusphoto@hotmail.com

Jeffrey Jacobs

Architectural Photography, Inc.

740 Dickinson

Memphis, TN 38107

(901) 274-7632

www.archphotoinc.com

Sam Mitchell

145 South Sappington Road

St. Louis, MO 63122

(314) 965-8051

Resources

Jamie Padgett
Padgett and Company
3001 West Jerome Street
Chicago, IL 60645
(773) 508-5846
www.padgettandco.com

Claudio Santini
12915 Greene Avenue
Los Angeles, CA 90066
(310) 578-7919
www.claudiosantini.com

Patrick Sudmeier
Pat Sudmeier Photography
512 Lake Court
Basalt, CO 81621
(970) 927-1320
sudmeier@rof.net

Wayne Thom
2458 Robert Road
Rowland Heights, CA 91748
(909) 595-6671

Architects/Designers

Anni Tilt and David Arkin, AIA
Arkin Tilt Architects
1062 Stannage Avenue
Albany, CA 94706
(510) 528-9830
info@arkintilt.com
www.arkintilt.com

Jeff Blackledge
Archimania PC
356 South Main Street
Memphis, TN 38103
(901) 527-3560
www.archimania.com

Ross Chapin, AIA, John
Prietto, Eric Richmond,
Matthew Swett
Ross Chapin Architects
P.O. Box 230
Langley, WA 98260
(360) 221-2373
www.rosschapin.com
www.cottagecompany.com

John Mike Cohen
Cohen Hilberry Architects
393 North Euclid Avenue,
Ste 340
St. Louis, MO 63108
(314) 367-8300

Marla Croke
Marla F. Croke Architecture,
Inc.
P.O. Box 2678
Telluride, CO 81435
(970) 728-1811

Scott Lindenau
Studio B Architects
555 North Mill Street
Aspen, CO 81611
(970) 920-9428
www.studiobarchitects.net

Brad Lynch
Brininstool + Lynch Architects
230 West Superior
Third Floor
Chicago, IL 60610
(312) 640-0505
www.brininstool-lynch.com

Steven Shortridge
Callas Shortridge Architects
3621 Hayden Avenue
Culver City, CA 90232
(310) 280-0404
www.callas-shortridge.com

Larry Yaw
Cottle Graybeal Yaw Architects
P.O. Box 529
Basalt, CO 81621
(970) 927-4925
www.cgyarchitects.com